Smart-Wiring Your Baby's Brain

Smart-Wiring Your Baby's Brain

What You Can Do to Stimulate Your Child During the Critical First Three Years

WINIFRED CONKLING

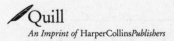

Quill

An Imprint of HarperCollins*Publishers*

NOTE: The information in this book applies to both boys and girls, but it can be cumbersome to shift back and forth between the pronouns "he" and "she" and "his" and "hers." To avoid this problem, feminine pronouns will be used throughout the volume.

HarperCollins books may be purchased for educational, business, or sales promotional use. For information please write: Special Markets Department, HarperCollins Publishers Inc., 10 East 53rd Street, New York, NY 10022.

FIRST EDITION

Designed by Jessica Shatan

Library of Congress Cataloging-in-Publication Data
Conkling, Winifred.
    Smart-wiring your baby's brain : what you can do to stimulate your child during the critical first three years / by Winifred Conkling.
      p.   cm.
    Includes bibliographical references.
    ISBN 0-380-80251-1
    1. Infants—Development.   2. Infants—Care.   3. Toddlers—Care.
4. Child rearing.   5. Brain—Growth.   I. Title.
HQ774 .C62 2001
649'.122—dc21   00-045859

01   02   03   04   05   ❖/RRD   10 9 8 7 6 5 4 3 2 1

For Hannah,
Ella, and
Gwendolyn

Contents

Introduction

For a parent, there is no greater accomplishment in the world than helping your child become the most intelligent, confident, trusting, and loving person she can be. While this goal may seem overwhelming at times, it need not be. In truth, your child will flourish and excel if you simply encourage her curiosity and celebrate her successes. Adults often forget the excitement and satisfaction of learning, but children find learning an absolute joy.

You are your child's first and most important teacher. Your efforts to provide an enriching and stimulating household environment can make a dramatic difference in your child's life. During the first three years of life, your child will develop the neurological foundation for her future intellectual growth. Your baby's brain will grow faster in the first year of life than at any other time. In fact, 70 percent of your child's brain development will be complete by the time she blows out her first birthday candle.

The effort you put into creating a wholesome and stimulating environment can allow your child to reach her ultimate potential. The first three years of your child's life will last forever. A child who might have been of average intelligence may become above average; the child who might have been of above-average intelligence may exhibit extraordinary gifts. Evidence suggests that by stimulating your baby's brain, you can add as much as 20 to 40 points to her IQ score.

Of course, your goal should not be to turn your child into a prodigy or to make your two-year-old behave like a five-year-old. The objective of early learning and brain stimulation is to reinforce your child's intrinsic interest in the world. Children are born curious; they are open to new experiences and eager to learn. Children soak in knowledge joyfully when they are exposed to a positive and supportive environment.

To teach your child you don't have to lecture or drill her on basic skills. While there will be many occasions when you instruct your child by answering questions or explaining new concepts, most of the time your job as a teacher should be to provide opportunities for your baby to explore, to touch, to play, to test, to succeed, and sometimes to fail—all within a safe environment.

Children learn best when they discover things for themselves. Researchers have repeatedly found that children's self-directed discoveries often prove to be better learning experiences than parent-directed activities. Your mission should be to set the scene for learning, then step aside and allow your child's natural abilities to take over.

PUTTING EARLY LEARNING TO THE TEST

By the time a child is ready for school, her intellectual potential has already been shaped by her home environment for better or for worse. Because early learning is so important to long-term intellectual achievement, a number of federal, state, and local programs have been developed to provide a healthy learning environment for children, especially those from disadvantaged backgrounds. The best known are those programs that receive federal funding through Head Start.

Over the years, dozens of long-term studies have documented the significant achievements of the children who participate in Head Start and other early-learning programs. Researchers have found that compared with children from similar backgrounds who did not participate in early-learning programs, those children who took part had higher IQ scores—from 7 to 10 points in several studies to as much as 30 points in another. Researchers also found that many more of the children in early-learning programs scored at grade level in reading and math and fewer failed in school or had to repeat a grade.

The most impressive results occurred among children who participated in the Home Start Program. This program focused on children under age three and attempted to provide an enriched home environment instead of simply a stimulating school setting. As part of Home Start, a teacher regularly visited the home and taught the mothers how to play developmentally appropriate games with their babies and toddlers.

Another project, the New Parents as Teachers Project in

St. Louis, Missouri, began training parents before their children were born. The parents who participated in this program represented a broad cross section of socioeconomic and social backgrounds. Again, trained teachers visited the homes and discussed with the parents ways to enrich their children's development. Parents were given packets of materials, directions for learning games, and detailed information on child development from birth to age three. The parents met in small groups to offer support and encouragement for their efforts.

Independent researchers compared the New Parents as Teachers Project children at age three with those who did not participate in the program. Not surprisingly, the children from the enriched environment scored significantly higher in all measures of intelligence, including auditory comprehension, verbal ability, and language ability, than did children from less intellectually stimulating homes. Clearly, early-learning experiences provide the intellectual foundation for later educational achievements.

YOUR HOME AS A CLASSROOM

While the demonstrable successes of these programs are inspiring, you don't need to join a formal program or enroll your child in infant enrichment classes to take advantage of the benefits of early education. Instead, you can use the advice in this book to provide appropriate stimulation during the first three years of your child's life.

Smart-Wiring Your Baby's Brain offers specific, prescriptive advice on what you can do to stimulate your child's brain development and boost her intelligence during early childhood. The recommendations are clearly stated, followed by an explanation of why a particular approach tends to be effective.

If you are the parent of a toddler or older child, don't despair about the lost opportunities for intellectual stimulation in infancy. While you cannot make up for lost time, your child will benefit from an enriched environment at any age or stage of development. Your child has not been irreparably damaged if she was not sung to in the womb or rocked for hours every evening after birth. Intellectual development is a lifelong process that actually begins before birth. It is never too late to encourage learning and to make new discoveries with your child. As human beings, we will never cease to learn and to grow, if given the chance.

Smart-Wiring Your Baby's Brain

1·Fertile Minds

How the Brain Is Wired for Learning

A mind stretched to a new idea never returns to its original dimensions.

—OLIVER WENDELL HOLMES,
nineteenth-century writer and physician

A baby's brain cells begin to grow three weeks after conception. These cells then multiply faster than any other cells in the body. This astonishing rate of brain growth continues throughout early childhood. At birth, a child's brain is about 25 percent of its adult weight; by age two the brain weighs fully 75 percent of its adult weight.

While the brain grows at a relatively predictable rate in healthy children, intelligence itself—what the brain can actually do—is neither predictable nor predetermined. Your child's intelligence can be changed—either for better or for worse—by the environment and experiences you provide for your child in the first three years.

Research has established that the brain needs appropriate

stimulation at certain critical periods of development to mature and fulfill its potential. This concept of critical periods has been demonstrated by animal research. Consider the experiments done on kittens who were blindfolded for four days during the second month of life. Researchers found that these animals were permanently blind because certain cells in their visual cortex were not activated at the appropriate time during their brain development.

Of course, it is harder to investigate critical periods in humans, but experience shows us that they exist. For example, we know that babies born with cataracts on their eyes will develop normal or almost normal vision if the cataracts are removed before the babies reach the age of two months, but if the surgery is delayed—particularly past the age of six months—vision is permanently impaired. Like the blindfolded kittens, children who do not receive adequate visual stimulation at the appropriate times do not develop normal vision.

Studies done on children who were reared in orphanages further illustrate the importance of environment. A classic study conducted more than thirty years ago by Dr. Wayne Dennis, a former professor of psychology at Brooklyn College of the City University of New York, examined the impact of the environment on children living in three orphanages in Tehran, Iran.

At one facility the infants were kept flat on their backs in individual cribs. They were not moved, held, snuggled, or massaged. They did not even spend time on their stomachs until they learned how to roll over on their own. The babies were fed using propped-up bottles; the older children were fed semisolid food by an overworked employee who did not take time for nurturing conversation. The children had no toys; they did not have an opportunity for any kind of recreation or play. Once the babies could sit alone, they were lined up on a piece of linoleum on the floor or positioned on a bench with a bar across the front to prevent them from falling. At the age of three, the children were moved to a second orphanage but the conditions were no better.

Not surprisingly, the researchers found that these neglected children experienced serious developmental delays. Of the children between the ages of one and two, fewer than half could sit up and only one could walk. (In comparison, almost all healthy children in the United States can sit on their own by the age of nine months.) Of the two-year-olds in the orphanage, less than half could stand, even when holding on to a chair or a hand, and less than 10 percent could walk. By the time they reached age three, only 15 percent had learned to walk.

The researchers also looked at a third group of children who stayed at an orphanage for children who were believed to be retarded. At this facility, the children received far more personal care and attention. They were held during feedings and given toys to play with. As a result of the contact and stimulation, these children—who were considered to be retarded—developed more skills than the normal, healthy children at the other facilities. All of the two-year-olds at the third facility could sit up, creep, and walk holding on to a hand or other support. Clearly, the environment dramatically altered the physical and mental development of these children.

While few children in the United States are forced to

endure the magnitude of deprivation and neglect that the researchers found in the Tehran facilities, not every child receives the kind of intellectual and emotional stimulation she deserves in early childhood. The consequences of intellectual impoverishment can be devastating. Researchers have found that early stimulation can actually alter the size, structure, and chemical functioning of the brain. Experiments with rats, dogs, cats, monkeys, and other animals have shown that animals become more intelligent when properly stimulated in infancy, compared with animals that do not receive the added stimulation, and their brains grow more rapidly. The more stimulation the animals received and the earlier they received it, the more intelligent they became.

Of course, intelligence is not entirely a matter of environment and early stimulation. A child may inherit a genetic predisposition toward certain skills or talents, such as those in music and mathematics. Natural ability is no guarantee of future success; environmental stimulation and appropriate training may be required to fully develop these inherent talents. An average child may be able to become a proficient musician with training, but a child with natural musical ability may be able to become a gifted musician with the same training and experience. The challenge as a parent is to discover and reinforce your child's natural abilities.

Even geniuses such as Mozart, Einstein, and Shakespeare would have been destined to a life of mediocrity and unfulfilled promise if they had been raised in environments like those found in the Tehran orphanages. Nature will provide your child with the potential for growth and achievement, but it's up to you to provide an environment that will allow your child to grow and to flourish.

THE MECHANICS OF THE BRAIN

The brain is unimaginably complex. Experts estimate that the two-pound organ consists of about 200 billion neurons. Each of these neurons connects to about five thousand of its neighbors, representing about one quadrillion neural connections. These neurons connect in specific ways that allow them to communicate. Each neuron consists of three parts: the cell body, the dendrites, and the axon. The cell body contains the cell nucleus; it is the core of the cell. Stemming from the cell body are branches or dendrites (*dendron* is the Greek word meaning tree). Also growing from the cell body is a long, sometimes branched fiber or tube known as an axon. In some cases (such as along the spinal cord), the axon from a single cell can extend several feet. At the end of the axon the neurons form synapses or connections with other neurons. The axons transmit the signals and the dendrites receive them.

Through these connections, neurons transmit their electrical and biochemical signals from cell to cell. In general, the more dendrites and connections you have in your brain, the greater your intellectual capacity. These additional dendrites allow the brain to make, communicate, or process information in a number of ways, speeding the connections and facilitating more complex thinking.

These billions of neurons in the brain have all formed by the end of the second trimester of pregnancy. In addition to the neurons, the infant's brain consists of about one trillion nerve cells known as the glia. (These cells are named after the Greek word for glue.) The glia form a honeycomb coating that protects and nourishes every neuron. Eventually, these cells surround the neurons with sheaths of a white, waxy substance called myelin. The glia will continue to develop throughout life, and they will contribute to the physical growth of the brain in early childhood.

Interestingly, a newborn has far more neurons and neural connections than an adult does. In fact, the brain doesn't need all of these neurons and about half of the neurons present at birth wither and die in early childhood. Those neurons that survive go on to form thousands of synapses, but many of these will also vanish during childhood as part of a complex process known as neural pruning. The pruning process allows the brain to become organized. Much of this pruning and neural organization takes place during the first two years of life.

This process of brain development illustrates the plasticity, or adaptability, of the human brain. Your child's brain will literally be shaped—it will form certain neural connections and eliminate others—in response to environment and experience. This process of neural pruning may seem cumbersome and unnecessary, but it makes sense from a biological point of view. The brain starts out with excess neurons so that it is ready for anything; an infant's brain is prepared for almost any type of sensory or motor stimulation. Those neural circuits that remain unused are discarded by the body, while those that are activated survive and grow stronger. This pruning process makes the brain more efficient; neurons that are stimulated grow new dendrite spines, until they eventually look like a heavily branched tree rather than a bare twig.

Every time your baby touches your face or listens to you sing a lullaby, electric charges ricochet through her brain, establishing certain neural circuits. The more a given pathway is used, the more established it becomes and the easier it is for information to travel along the pathway. Your child's brain development is not simply a natural process that will unfold over time while you stand by idly and watch; it is a biological process that is guided by the flood of sensory experiences your child encounters every day.

THE ENRICHED BRAIN

For more than fifty years, researchers have been trying to discover exactly how experience affects brain development and intelligence. One early study looked at the impact of light on the development of vision in chimpanzees. The researchers reared a group of chimps in the dark for periods up to sixteen months; the animals raised in darkness experienced atrophy of the retina and the neurons in the optic nerve. The atrophy was reversible during the first seven months, but it led to total blindness after one year. Those neurons for sight that were not stimulated during the first year of life degenerated and ultimately disappeared.

Studies like this demonstrated that a lack of stimulation can impair neural development. But investigators then asked a follow-up question: if neurons can be impaired by a lack of stimulation, can they also be enhanced by exposure to an enriched or stimulating environment? Many researchers have proved that the answer is yes.

In one study, just after weaning, rat pups were placed in

either an "enriched" or an "impoverished" cage for eighty days. The enriched environment included ten to twelve rats in a spacious cage with plenty of food, water, and toys, including ladders, platforms, boxes, and exercise wheels. The toys were changed daily so that the rats did not become bored. They also got their chance to run the mazes and explore new situations on a daily basis.

The impoverished rats, on the other hand, spent their time alone in cages with solid walls offering no visual stimulation. They had no access to toys or noise and were kept in a dimly lit room. To minimize the role of genetics, each rat in the enriched environment had a littermate in the impoverished environment.

After eighty days, all of the animals were euthanized and their brains were weighed and analyzed. Compared with the rats in the impoverished environment, the rats in the enriched environment had brains with a heavier cerebral cortex (the part of the brain that controls learning, perception, and memory); they also had larger neurons and a more intricate network of neural connections. Later researchers who conducted similar studies found that the brains of stimulated rats contain as much as 25 percent more synapses per neuron.

The findings also hold true for humans. Researchers at Baylor College of Medicine have found that children who don't play much or are rarely touched develop brains that are actually 20 to 30 percent smaller than normal for their age. (Because high-tech scanners are used to take these measurements, the children are not harmed in any way.) Rich and stimulating environments produce enriched and stimulated brains.

THE GROWTH OF THE BRAIN

An enriched environment encourages brain development, but it cannot force the brain to grow faster than Mother Nature intended. Some sections of the brain are well developed at birth, while others are quite primitive. At birth, the most well developed sections of the brain are the brain stem and the midbrain, which control reflexes, states of consciousness, and vital bodily functions, such as respiration and elimination. The midbrain is surrounded by the cerebrum and cerebral cortex, which control voluntary movement, perception, and intellectual functions, such as learning, thinking, and communicating.

The first parts of the cerebrum to mature are the areas that control simple motor activity (such as moving the arms and legs) and those that involve the senses (seeing, hearing, smelling, and tasting). As parents of infants are well aware, newborns are highly reflexive, and this is because the reflexes are controlled by the most developed areas of a newborn's brain. These reflexes are biological survival aids, designed to protect the infant. These behaviors are not learned, and in fact they are unlearned or overshadowed as the brain develops a more sophisticated system of behavior.

By six months of age, the child's brain has grown and developed more sophistication in the area of primary motor activity; by this age, the infant can control many of her physical gestures and activities. At this same age, some of the inborn reflexes begin to disappear. In essence, the higher centers of the brain are supplanting the more primitive and instinctive areas of the brain.

As the various areas of the brain develop, the brain cells

begin the process of myelinization. The glial cells produce a waxy, fatty substance known as myelin, which covers and protects the individual neurons. The myelin coating acts like the insulation over telephone wires; it helps to speed the neural impulses through the cells, allowing the neurons to communicate more efficiently and directly. The myelin also helps prevent the crossing of the electrical signals from one neuron to another.

The myelinization of the nerves occurs in a sequence that correlates with the development of the nervous system. At birth, a child's sensory pathways are fairly well myelinated (she can hear, smell, taste, feel, and see fairly well). As the child grows and becomes more capable of voluntary movement (she lifts her head, rolls over, learns to stand, takes her first steps) her physical accomplishments follow the pattern of myelinization of various neural pathways.

Myelinization occurs quickly in the first three years of life, though some parts of the brain do not become fully myelinated until early adulthood. The part of the brain that allows for prolonged concentration is not fully myelinated until at least puberty, which explains why most young children have short attention spans.

Without myelinization, people lose control of their muscles. People suffering from multiple sclerosis experience a gradual loss of the myelin surrounding their neurons. The cause of multiple sclerosis is unknown, and its symptoms depend on the nerves that are affected. Over time, the person suffering from the disease loses muscular control and may become paralyzed; in many cases the condition is fatal.

Reflexes and Responses

When your child is born, most of her movements are based on reflexes. Over several months, as her brain matures, the reflexive movement is replaced by voluntary, intentional movement.

If you . . .   make a loud noise

Your child . . .   will reach her arms out, throw her head back, and close her eyes (Moro reflex)

This disappears . . .   at two to three months

If you . . .   tap the bridge of her nose

Your child . . .   will close her eyes tightly

This disappears . . .   at one to two months

If you . . .   straighten her arm at the elbows or legs at the knees

Your child . . .   will flex her arms and legs

This disappears . . .   at three months

If you . . .   hold her under her arms and let her soles touch a flat surface

Your child . . .   will place one foot in front of the other and "walk"

This disappears . . .   at two months

If you . . .   put her on her stomach

Your child . . .   will turn her head to the side, lift her head slightly, and make a swimming-like motion with her arms and legs

This disappears . . .   at two months

If you . . .   place her on her back and gently turn her head from side to side

Your child . . .   will extend her arm on the side her head is turned to and flex the other arm at the shoulder

This disappears . . .   at two to four months

If you . . .   stroke the top of her foot or hand

Your child . . .   will withdraw her foot or hand

This disappears . . .   at two to three months

If you . . .   stroke the palm of her hand or the sole of her foot

Your child . . .   will grasp with the hand or foot

This disappears . . .   at two to five months

If you . . .   stroke the outside of her foot

Your child . . .	will spread her toes and her big toe will go upward
This disappears . . .	at one to two months
If you . . .	stroke her cheek
Your child . . .	will turn her head toward the side that is stroked (rooting reflex)
This disappears . . .	at four months
If you . . .	place an object over her face
Your child . . .	will twist her head, flail her arms, and make every attempt to remove the object
This disappears . . .	at six months

A Timetable for Brain Growth

---

3 weeks after conception: The brain cells begin to form.

10 to 18 weeks after conception: The number of brain cells is established, but the cells will continue to develop.

20 weeks after conception: The brain enters a growth spurt that will last until age two; the neurons increase in size; some dendrites branch and grow, while others are "pruned" away.

20 weeks after conception: The process of mylenization begins and continues at a rapid pace until age four.

At birth: The newborn's brain is 25 percent of its adult weight.

At 6 months: The infant's brain is 50 percent of its adult weight.

At 1 year: The infant's brain is 70 percent of its adult weight.

At 3 years: The child's brain is more than 90 percent of its adult weight.

HOW WE LEARN

When your child learns something new, this information is not neatly filed away in a single part of her brain. Many different parts of the brain are used to learn a single concept. For example, a simple concept such as "my blue shirt" may be stored in many different parts of the brain. It could be stored with the neurons about clothes, about blue things, about things in the closet, or about birthday gifts. You could trigger a memory about the blue shirt by stimulating any one of those parts of the brain. This concept is known as multiple mapping.

Multiple mapping shows us that memory involves the entire brain, and that for memory and recall to work properly, the brain's neural network must work efficiently. It also means it is difficult to destroy a memory since it is filed away or stored in many disparate parts of the brain. What your child really learns and stores in her brain is apt to be with her for life.

In order for information to be stored by the brain, it must be experienced. Most learning involves one of three primary techniques—seeing (visual memory: studying a map), hearing (auditory memory: listening to a lecture), or doing (kinesthetic memory: riding a bike or tying your shoes). Almost everything we learn and every memory we have fall into one of these categories. Each of these memories is stored in a different part of the brain. Visual memories reside in the right side of the brain's cortex, auditory memories reside in the left side, and kinesthetic memories are stored in the cerebellum.

Most people tend to be more efficient at one type of memory than another. About 65 percent of all people learn best using visual memory, 20 percent learn best using auditory memory, and about 15 percent learn best using kinesthetic memory.

You can sometimes tell what type of memory a person uses most by listening to how she describes things. People who use detailed visual imagery are visual learners; those who can recall conversations or things they heard tend to be auditory learners. People who recall memories in terms of how an experience felt probably lean toward kinesthetic memory. People with exceptional memories may have highly developed skills in all three types of learning. Because they store memories in several different ways, they are able to access that memory using several sections of the brain.

In general, visual learners pick up new material more quickly than auditory or kinesthetic learners, and they tend to be more confident in what they learn. However, they often learn too much irrelevant information and confuse the order of things. Auditory learners are good at compartmentalizing complex material, but they seem to lack confidence in their memories (even though their memories tend to be just as accurate as the memories of visual learners).

Kinesthetic learning is not appropriate for most academic subjects, but it tends to be the most long-lasting type of memory. For example, we've all heard that once you learn to ride a bike, you never forget how. One of the reasons why kinesthetic memory endures is that it is located in the cerebellum, which is a part of the brain less vulnerable to the degenerative effects of Alzheimer's disease and other brain disorders. Even people with advanced Alzheimer's may remember how to play the piano without forgetting a note or knit a sweater without dropping a stitch, even though they may not recognize their spouse of fifty years.

Another unusual feature about kinesthetic memory is that it works best when you don't think about it. The more you ponder the physical demands of riding a bike—or playing the piano or hitting a golf ball—the less capable you are of doing it well. For this reason, athletes often try to clear their minds and enter a meditative state before competition.

You can try to stimulate your child's learning by using the type of learning that works best for your child. In addition, you can try to strengthen the memory in other parts of your child's brain by reinforcing the lesson using all the learning styles. For example, have your child see the material, discuss it with her, and if appropriate have her experience it in a hands-on fashion by holding an object, tracing her finger over a shape, or manipulating a puzzle piece. In this way, the experience and memory will be recorded in the maximum number of ways possible.

PROVIDING YOUR BABY WITH AN ENRICHED CHILDHOOD

The typical American child does not live in an enriched environment. She passively watches three or four hours of television; she plays with toys that undermine creativity and self-directed play; she spends little time reading, writing, or engaging in imaginative play.

In an attempt to better understand how to enrich a child's environment, researchers have studied the way that mothers interact with their children. The findings of these studies are remarkably consistent: for children to reach their intellectual potential, they need opportunities for exploration and play, they need to be able to choose to study subjects that interest them, and they need to be surrounded by encouraging and supportive people who love them.

The following points also make a difference in child development:

- Children need the consistent attention of a loving adult caregiver.

- The caregiver needs to respond with friendly and affirming words to a child's attempts at communication.

- The caregiver needs to avoid expressions of anger and physical punishment.

- The caregiver needs to take an interest in the child's activities.

- The child needs to spend time in a safe and secure environment.

- The child needs regular contact with adults.

- The child needs age-appropriate toys and art materials.

- The child needs opportunities for regular outings and new things to look at.

- The child needs to be read to at least three times a week by the age of six months.

Fortunately, you have an opportunity to enhance your child's intellectual development by offering her an enriched environment during the critical period from birth to age three. The younger your child, the greater the influence her environment has on her and the greater your opportunities to stimulate her intelligence. The material described in the remaining chapters of this book will offer specific suggestions on ways to enhance your child's intelligence.

2·In the Beginning

Enhancing Your Child's Brain in the Womb

Your child's first nine months of life—the period between conception and birth—can have a profound effect on her brain development and long-term intellectual potential. If you drink alcohol, take over-the-counter and prescription drugs, use illicit drugs or are exposed to lead and other toxins, you can impair the normal development of your growing child. On the other hand, you can provide a stimulating and enriching fetal environment for your child that can actually jump-start neural development. This chapter will summarize key ways in which you can protect your child and enhance her mental development even before she is born.

PROTECTING YOUR BABY IN THE WOMB

Avoid the use of all over-the-counter and prescription drugs without a doctor's expressed recommendation.
The risks of taking medications during pregnancy can best be illustrated by the infamous thalidomide tragedy. The

drug was marketed as a mild over-the-counter tranquilizer that was also helpful in the treatment of morning sickness associated with pregnancy. When it was introduced, thalidomide had been tested on pregnant rats, with no complications, but it had not been tested on humans.

The horrific birth defects caused by the drug became rapidly apparent. Thousands of women who took thalidomide during their first trimester of pregnancy delivered babies with a number of birth defects, including fused fingers and toes; deformed eyes, ears, noses, and hearts; and a structural problem in which either the limbs were missing or the feet and hands were attached to the torso like flippers.

Researchers soon learned that certain defects were associated with the use of thalidomide during specific time frames. For example, mothers who took the drug on or near the twenty-first day after conception tended to give birth to children without ears. Those who took the drug on the twenty-fifth to the twenty-seventh day of pregnancy often had children with deformed or missing arms. However, if a woman used the drug after the fortieth day of pregnancy, in most cases the child suffered no ill effects. The impact of the drug was directly linked to certain stages of fetal development.

While the thalidomide catastrophe should make pregnant women pause before taking any medications without a doctor's recommendation, at least 60 percent of all pregnant women take at least one prescription or over-the-counter drug during their pregnancy. Talk to your obstetrician before taking *any* medicine. Keep in mind that even commonly used and seemingly innocuous drugs, such as aspirin, have been linked to developmental problems and neonatal bleeding when used at high doses.

Of course, not every drug will put your baby at risk. Discuss with your obstetrician which medicines can be safely taken during pregnancy and which should be avoided. Also, be sure to let all your health care practitioners know that you are pregnant before receiving treatment or taking any medications.

Do not consume alcohol while pregnant.
When Mom drinks alcohol, so does her baby. While a glass or two of white zinfandel may not make Mom feel tipsy, it can have a more significant impact on her baby. The baby's liver is not able to filter the alcohol as effectively as the mother's can, so the alcohol circulates in the baby's bloodstream twice as long as it does in the mother's, causing a greater degree of cellular damage.

Excessive use of alcohol during pregnancy—the consumption of about five or six drinks a day of wine, beer, or distilled spirits—can cause a condition known as fetal alcohol syndrome. Babies born with this condition tend to have small heads and malformed hearts, limbs, joints, and faces. They may be irritable, hyperactive, and prone to tremors or seizures—and, not surprisingly, they tend to have below-average intelligence. In addition, mothers who drink to excess stand a greater risk of miscarrying, delivering prematurely, and experiencing complications during labor and delivery.

The risks of drinking are dose related, meaning that the more a woman drinks, the greater the risk to her baby and the more severe the symptoms are likely to be. However, even moderate drinking can pose problems. Drinking just one to three ounces of alcohol a day—the equivalent of one to three glasses of wine, mugs of beer, or mixed drinks—can cause a milder version of the syndrome known as fetal alcohol effects. In these cases, babies often experience delayed physical growth, poor motor skills, difficulty paying attention, and subnormal intellectual abilities. Even women who drink less than an ounce of alcohol a day are more likely than nondrinkers to have babies with below-average intelligence.

Unlike the damage caused by thalidomide, which occurred during certain stages of fetal development, the adverse effects of alcohol are not limited to a specific period of gestation. In other words, drinking late in pregnancy can be just as damaging to the baby as drinking during the first trimester. Don't worry about any alcohol you may have consumed before you knew you were pregnant, but you should avoid alcohol altogether during your pregnancy.

For More Information

If you would like to stop drinking during pregnancy but find it difficult to quit, contact one of the following groups for help:

ALCOHOLICS ANONYMOUS
(212) 870-3400, or check the Yellow Pages for your local listing

RATIONAL RECOVERY
(916) 621-4374

SECULAR ORGANIZATIONS FOR SOBRIETY (SOS)
(716) 834-2922

Don't smoke cigarettes during pregnancy and avoid smoke-filled rooms.

While there is little reason to believe that smoking can cause congenital malformations, there are scores of studies showing that smoking slows the rate of fetal growth and increases the risk of miscarriage during pregnancy. It also can cause abnormal placental implantation, premature placental detachment, premature rupture of membranes, and early delivery. In fact, an estimated 14 percent of premature deliveries in the United States are related to cigarette smoking.

The health risks posed by smoking during pregnancy don't cease when the baby is born. Studies have found that children of women who smoke are more likely than babies of nonsmokers to suffer from apnea (breathing lapses) and sudden infant death syndrome (SIDS). Some studies have found that children of smokers are more likely to be hyperactive and to experience learning problems in school than children of nonsmokers.

Smoking interferes with the exchange of oxygen and nutrients between the mother and the baby. This diminished oxygen supply can impair the baby's brain development. When you smoke, your baby's heartbeat races and her body receives a reduced supply of oxygen through the placenta. In essence, your child experiences carbon monoxide poisoning. The more cigarettes a woman smokes, the greater the risks, but the baby can be at risk even if Mom is simply a passive smoker who inhales smoke from the environment. Avoid smoke-filled areas.

Fortunately, there is no evidence that smoking before pregnancy puts your child at risk as long as you kick the habit before getting pregnant. The risks to the developing fetus are greatest after the fourth month, so make every effort to stop smoking by that point. To give your child every opportunity to reach her potential, avoid exposure to cigarette smoke throughout pregnancy (and do not allow your child to be exposed to smoke after she is born).

For More Information

If you need help giving up cigarettes, consider contacting the following organization:

SMOKENDERS
4455 East Camelback Road, Suite D-150
Phoenix, AZ 85018
(602) 840-7414

Avoid exposure to environmental lead.
Lead is one of the most important environmental threats to your child's intelligence. Lead accumulates in the body, causing brain damage and harming other organs. Exposure to lead increases a woman's risk of developing pregnancy-induced hypertension and raises the potential of serious neurological and behavioral problems for her child.

Lead poisoning usually occurs gradually, over several weeks or months. The symptoms usually include irritability, digestive system problems, and fatigue. Severe lead poisoning can be fatal.

Lead can be found in the air (from automobile exhaust), old paint, water, and the soil.

air: While levels of lead in the air have dropped dramatically since the U.S. Environmental Protection Agency mandated the use of unleaded gasoline, it is still a significant risk factor since it is found in diesel gasoline. Airborne lead can easily travel two hundred feet from a roadway, so avoid walking or exercising near heavily traveled roads during pregnancy, and do not allow your child to play outdoors near busy roads after she is born.

old paint: Before 1978, lead was a common ingredient in household paint, especially white and yellow shades. Since then it has been banned, but leaded paint chips and dust are quite common in older homes. If you live in a home containing pre-1978 paint, be cautious during renovations or home-repair projects.

water: The water in many homes and municipal water supplies contains lead that leaches from the solder joining the pipes. (The problem is especially common in areas with acidic or low-pH water.) To minimize lead levels, let the water run for one minute in the morning before drinking it or using it for cooking. You may want to have your water tested in a lab; local testing facilities should be listed in the Yellow Pages, or contact your board of health. You may also choose to use a water filter or to drink bottled water, especially during pregnancy.

soil: Lead tends to linger in the soil after it accumulates from automobile exhaust or flakes from windows. Be cautious of lead in the soil when gardening during pregnancy.

Once your child is born, make a special effort to mini-mize her exposure to these lead sources. Be sure to have your child's blood lead levels tested at one year. Discuss your concerns about lead with your pediatrician.

For More Information

If you want to know more about lead poisoning during pregnancy and early childhood, contact the following organization:

ALLIANCE TO END CHILDHOOD LEAD POISONING
227 Massachusetts Avenue, NE, Suite 200
Washington, DC 20002
(202) 543-1147

Avoid exposure to radiation.
The devastating effects of radiation on fetal development became clear following the 1945 atomic explosions in Japan. Not a single pregnant woman within a half mile of the blasts gave birth to a live child. Seventy-five percent of the pregnant women within a mile and a quarter of the explosions gave birth to seriously deformed children, most of whom died soon after birth. All of those who lived were mentally retarded.

While most pregnant women don't experience such intense exposures to radiation, even low doses can present health problems. Measuring the hazards associated with radiation exposure is difficult, because radiation harm may not show up until years after a child is born. For example, a child exposed to radiation who appears normal can suffer a higher than normal risk of developing cancer later in life.

To protect your child (and yourself), avoid X rays and exposure to radiation whenever possible during your pregnancy, particularly X rays of the pelvis and abdomen. Be sure to notify your dentist of your pregnancy so that you can delay any elective X rays until after your baby is born.

Minimize your daily stress.

When a pregnant woman becomes stressed or emotionally excited, her endocrine glands secrete adrenaline and other powerful hormones. These hormones make their way into the fetal bloodstream, where they rev up the baby's motor activity.

Short-term stressful situations, such as a fall, a scary movie, or a fight with a spouse or partner, won't cause any long-lasting problems for mother or child. However, ongoing severe stress can cause miscarriages, lengthy labors, and premature and low-birth-weight babies. Infants whose mothers were stressed-out during pregnancy tend to be irritable, hyperactive, and irregular in their eating, sleeping, and bowel habits.

Learn to control your daily stress through meditation, deep breathing, yoga, or therapy. Allow the anxieties of the day to pass through you so that you can remain calm and centered.

For More Information

If you want to know more about the impact of stress on the body and the techniques you can use to ease stress, contact the following organization:

AMERICAN INSTITUTE OF STRESS
124 Park Avenue
Yonkers, NY 10703
(914) 963-1200

Don't eat any undercooked meat or handle any cat that may be a source of toxoplasmosis infection.
A healthy adult can fight off the toxoplasmosis organism with little more than a short-lived rash, cough, swollen glands, and other coldlike symptoms. If a pregnant woman is infected with toxoplasmosis, she will recover from the illness, but her baby may remain infected until after birth. Approximately one out of five babies with toxoplasmosis suffers from mental retardation, epilepsy, eye damage, hearing loss, and hydrocephalus (water on the brain).

Most cases of toxoplasmosis can be traced to eating raw or undercooked red meat or to exposure to the feces of a cat infected with the disease. The organism can't survive temperatures above 140 degrees Fahrenheit, so be sure to cook meat to at least this temperature. (If you're dining in a restaurant, order your food well done.)

Toxoplasmosis can also be caused by organisms living in the digestive tracts of cats. Household disinfectants can't kill the organisms, and they can remain infectious for up to one year, especially in moist soil or water. (Cats usually pick up the bug by eating raw meat, rodents, or birds, or by being exposed to an infected cat.) If you have a cat, minimize your risk of infection by having someone else clean the litter box during your pregnancy. You might want to have your cat tested by a veterinarian to find out if it has the infection. If your cat is healthy, try to avoid new exposures to the disease by not allowing the animal to roam outside, where the risk of contracting the disease is the greatest.

ENRICHING YOUR BABY IN THE WOMB

Talk to your baby.

Your baby can get to know you and become familiar with your voice before you meet face-to-face on her birthday. Research shows that babies who are talked to regularly in utero tend to lift their heads to look for the familiar speaker when they meet their loving parents for the first time.

During pregnancy you may want to help your child become familiar with your voice by speaking directly to her for ten minutes or so each day. You may also want to create a recording of your voice (or your spouse's voice) that can be played to Mom's abdomen once or twice a day from the seventh month on. Parents should use a loving singsong or baby voice when addressing their child. Refer to the child by name (if you've picked out a name and know the sex) and identify yourself as "Mommy" and "Daddy."

If creating an audiocassette seems too involved, consider reading to your unborn child. Research done at the University of North Carolina at Greensboro found that babies recognize books read to them before birth. As part of a study, sixteen pregnant women were asked to read aloud *The Cat in the Hat* twice a day for the last six and a half weeks of pregnancy. By the time of their birth, the infants had heard the story read for about five hours. After birth, each baby heard a tape of her mother reading first *The Cat in the Hat,* then another poem. A sucking test showed that the babies consistently preferred the familiar volume, *The Cat in the Hat.*

Stroke your baby.
Get in touch with your baby before she is born by touching and stroking her in the womb. From the thirteenth to the twenty-seventh week, stroke your abdomen lightly from below up to the belly button. By the twenty-eighth week, ask your doctor about the baby's position so that you can stroke from her head to her toes. The stroking enhances the development of her neuromuscular pathways.

Get rocking.
The gentle stimulation created by rocking back and forth in a rocking chair can help to develop the part of your baby's brain that is linked to the balance mechanisms of the inner ear. This part of the brain also provides the foundation for language skills and other tasks of higher-order thinking that develop later on.

Your baby's brain will respond to movement after about the fifth month, so get moving. Rock slowly, at about twenty rocks per minute. The motion should be soothing to both mother and child.

Genetics and Personality

When the big day arrives and you meet your little one for the first time, you may be surprised—either pleasantly or unpleasantly—by the personality of the little one you encounter. From the moment of birth, your child will exhibit personality traits. Throughout your child's life, her core temperament will determine whether she is nervous or easygoing, serious or carefree, meek or assertive.

Most of the experts who ponder the question of nature versus nurtrure now attribute about half of a child's personality to genetics and half to environmental factors. Researchers have found strong evidence of an inherited predisposition for certain personality traits, including aggression, depression, empathy, excitability, imagination, leadership, obsession, shyness, susceptibility to addiction, traditionalism, and vulnerability to stress.

When it comes to intelligence, the experts estimate that genetics and environment contribute equally to overall intellect. For example, if your child's IQ is 20 points above normal, you could attribute 10 points to genetics and 10 points to environment. Most researchers believe that the environment can encourage or inhibit certain genetic predispositions, but it cannot create traits that have no genetic basis.

Studies of identical twins (from a single egg) support this conclusion and provide insights into how environment influences behavior. If environment alone shapes behavior and personality, then twins reared together would be expected to be more similar than those separated at birth. Surprisingly, twins who grow up together are no more similar than those reared separately. Twins who grow up in different households show strong similarities, including religious preferences and career choices.

In one case, identical twin girls separated at birth and reared in separate homes were found to share remarkable similarities four years later. The adoptive parents of one of the girls reported that she was a finicky eater, stubborn and unco-operative, who would eat nothing unless it had cinnamon on it. The adoptive parents of the second girl said that she was a fantastic eater, compliant and cooperative, who would eat absolutely anything—as long as it had cinnamon on it.

Accept your child for who she is, even if her personality traits annoy you. After all, your child's behavior may be inher-ited—you have only yourself (and your spouse) to blame.

3 · The Joy of Learning

Successful Strategies for Teaching Your Child

Treat people as if they were what they
ought to be and you help them to become
what they're capable of being.

—JOHANN WOLFGANG VON GOETHE,
eighteenth-century German poet

Your child will eagerly absorb anything you tell her and
willingly participate in almost any learning activity
you choose for her—as long as the experience is fun. If you
show your child that learning is enjoyable, that life is exciting, that curiosity is rewarded with discovery, and that the
world is a positive place, then you will be going a long way
toward creating in your child a love of learning that will
last a lifetime.

Most real learning takes place within the context of
ordinary life. It does not require formal training; it is a natural consequence of daily experience. Learning does not
happen within a structured, orderly framework at a meas-

ured and predictable pace; it occurs in spurts, with one experience building on another.

APPRECIATE YOUR CHILD'S UNIQUE GIFTS

Every child is gifted. Some children earn high scores on IQ tests and other conventional measures of intelligence, while others exhibit skills and abilities that may be more difficult to measure. The traditional assessment of gifted-ness has been rethought in recent years in light of the work of Professor Howard Gardner at Harvard University.

Rather than relying on a single measure of intelligence, Gardner argues that there are at least seven basic types of intelligence: linguistic (verbal), spatial, bodily kinesthetic, musical, logical-mathematical, interpersonal (social), and intrapersonal (highly developed sense of self). According to Gardner, every child has all seven types of intelligence to differing degrees. By understanding which gifts your child has you can better encourage her learning and exploration.

Linguistic: Children with linguistic intelligence have a love for words and language. They learn best by see-ing, hearing, and saying words.

Spatial: Children with spatial intelligence tend to learn visually. They learn best by seeing pictures, pho-tographs, diagrams, maps, films, and other visual pre-sentations of information.

Bodily-Kinesthetic: Children with kinesthetic skills learn best through movement. They easily learn through role-playing, drama, dance, and other action-based learning experiences.

Musical: Children with musical gifts learn through the use of rhythm and melody. They learn best when information is sung, tapped out, or put to music.

Logical-Mathematical: Children with logical-mathematical skills think in terms of abstract patterns and relationships. They learn well using puzzles and games of logic.

Interpersonal: Children with gifts involving interpersonal relations learn best by relating to and cooperating with people. They thrive on group activities such as play groups and school clubs.

Intrapersonal: Children with intrapersonal skills learn best on their own. They do well with self-teaching computer programs and books that allow them to work independently.

These different types of intelligence reflect differences in neurological wiring in the brain, according to Gardner. For example, people with linguistic intelligence show a great deal of activity and development in the left hemisphere of the brain, and those with spatial intelligence show more development in the right side.

The traditional educational system is geared to recognize the accomplishments of verbal and logical children—those who excel in reading, spelling, reasoning, and computing. The special talents of children who are gifted in dance or leadership or overall creativity are often overlooked.

As a parent, you need to recognize and praise your child's gifts, even if they are not the skills or abilities you value most. You should encourage your child to develop her skills and to realize her potential, whether that means she will become a mathematician, a psychoanalyst, or a Shakespearean actor.

The Secrets of Successful Parenting

What makes an exceptional child turn into an exceptional adult? To find out, Professor Benjamin Bloom of the University of Chicago surveyed 120 Americans considered to be among the top mathematicians, sculptors, neurologists, swimmers, and tennis players in the country. He found that these accomplished adults all had parents who shared certain outlooks about rearing children, though none set out to produce a prodigy:

The parents encouraged their children to play and to explore the world. The children learned through play and had plenty of time to explore their own abilities and the environment around them.

The parents provided a stimulating and motivating home environment. The parents themselves were motivated and dedicated to their own interests, and they encouraged their children to follow their own interests. The children were encouraged to be curious and to ask questions, but they were not pushed into early academic training. In fact, six out of the twenty neurologists were actually slow in learning how to read.

The parents supported the children's self-chosen interest and made the children's passion a priority. The parents allowed the children to choose a direction and set a goal, and they encouraged and backed the children up in pursuit of the goal.

The parents encouraged independent thinking. They kept an open mind about their children's activities and encouraged them to think for themselves.

While following these strategies won't ensure that your child will cultivate an extraordinary talent that will put her at the top of her field, these approaches to parenting will help your child develop her skills and interests in a way that almost certainly will lead to her personal satisfaction and fulfillment.

STRATEGIES FOR A LIFETIME OF LEARNING

The strategies discussed in the rest of this chapter will not only help you be a better teacher but also help to create an environment that will be conducive to learning.

Keep it fun.

The more your child enjoys spending time with you as she explores the world, the more motivated she will be to learn and to experience more. Your enthusiasm for learning and adventure is contagious, so loosen up and look at the world through your child's eyes.

Delight in your toddler's successes.

Enthusiastically praising your child's little victories and big discoveries will delight her and stimulate her neurological development. In fact, between the ages of ten and eighteen months, praise strengthens the neurological connections between the frontal cortex and the part of the midbrain responsible for emotions. Children who are encouraged in their exploration will be "wired" to develop more interest in trying new experiences. On the other hand, toddlers whose achievements are ignored or criticized will not develop a strong neurological relationship between activity and emotional rewards, and they may be more hesitant to try new things as they get older.

Be sure your child is well rested.

Even avid explorers need naps. Your little one needs sleep to keep her brain working at its best and to minimize her mood swings. During sleep, the body recuperates from the day and the mind resolves conflicts and consolidates memories. Babies and toddlers have different sleep needs, but a regular bedtime routine can help them develop sound habits for sound sleep.

Keep in mind that the sleep patterns of infants and toddlers are different from those of adults. About half of an infant's sleep—six to nine hours daily—is rapid eye movement (REM) sleep, compared with less than two hours for the typical adult. During REM sleep the brain processes information, consolidates memories, and works on forming and pruning synapses in the brain. Your child needs plenty of sleep to prepare for the challenges of learning new information and to process and record the information learned during the previous day.

Be sure your child is in the mood for play.
Your child will be in no position to explore or to learn if she is tired, hungry, or not feeling well. The same thing goes for parents: don't feel obligated to interact with your child if you don't feel focused on the experience. Your child will be able to read your mood and will not be fooled by your distracted attempts to connect. It makes more sense to delay your play for an hour or so until both of you really feel like spending time together.

Does Your Baby Want to Play?

Your baby may not be able to speak to you, but she will offer physical cues as to whether or not she is paying attention or is overstimulated. Keep these warning signs in mind when playing with your child:

SIGNS OF APPROPRIATE STIMULATION
- Your child's breathing becomes slow and even.

- Your child's sucking rate slows down as she focuses on the source of stimulation.

- Your child's pupils dilate and her eyes widen.

- Your child's abdomen relaxes.

- Your child turns her head toward you or the stimulation.

- Your child looks at the source of stimulation for at least four to ten seconds (her attention span at birth).

- Your child's fingers and toes flare or fan toward you in excitement.

SIGNS OF OVERSTIMULATION

- Your child will cry and not be distracted by additional stimulation.

- Your child will squirm and flail her arms and legs.

- Your child will thrust out her tongue.

- Your child will open her eyes wide and stare into space.

- Your child will appear sleepy or even fall asleep to escape the stimulation.

Shhh. . . . Keep the noise down.

When you want to interact with your child, keep other distractions to a minimum. Turn off the television and radio; try to find a place that is quiet and free of chores or other things that will be distracting to you or your child.

Avoid the glare of bright lamps for the first few months.

Newborns see better in dimly lit rooms because their eyes can't adjust to the bright glare of a 100-watt lightbulb. Use 25- and 40-watt lightbulbs in the nursery and other rooms your child spends a lot of time in for the first three or four months. With the appropriate lighting, your child can focus on your face and interact with you without squinting or shielding her face from the glare. In fact, newborns tend to close their eyes or sleep when exposed to excessive light, and they are most alert when the lights are turned down.

Use the playpen sparingly.
Whenever possible, allow your child to have freedom of movement. You want your child to have an opportunity to look around and to explore, so minimize the time she is confined to a crib or a playpen during waking hours, especially if she cannot sit on her own.

Do it again and again and again . . .
Young children learn from repetition. A child masters an activity by repeating it; at the same time, she is programming and strengthening the neural pathways in her brain that are used to perform an activity. Allow—and even encourage—your child to repeat activities if they involve new skills she is developing.

Keep the nos to a minimum.
Your goal as a parent should be to create a safe and stimulating environment for your child. Your child should have as much freedom as possible, and this can be accomplished by baby-proofing your home and removing hazards. Of course, your child needs to be supervised and played with, but she does not need to hear incessant nagging—"Don't

touch that" or "That's not for babies." Too much scolding can dampen a child's curiosity about exploring the world.

Studies have found that parents who raise the most capable children baby-proof their homes so that their children are safe and breakables are out of harm's way. Once this is accomplished, the child can explore a room without restriction, and this diverse experience helps stimulate neural development. These broader boundaries and greater feelings of accomplishment can also minimize the stress and rebellion common during the terrible twos, when a child presses to establish her independence.

As your child gets older and becomes mobile, she can maintain her freedom if you teach her how to get out of troublesome situations. Show your child how to climb off the bed, how to back down from a chair, and how to safely inch her way down the stairs on her bottom.

Let learning be its own reward.
Don't feel compelled to offer your child stickers or toys or special treats to learn something new. Learning is exciting and it should be valued for its own sake. If you try to bribe your child with incentives, you are teaching her that knowledge is worth nothing without a prize.

Researchers at Brandeis University found that children who were promised a reward if they told a story or made a collage were less creative than those who participated solely for the challenge and feeling of accomplishment. Instead of offering your child an external incentive for learning, reinforce and share with her the feelings of accomplishment and pride when she learns something new. In the long run, these personal feelings will be a much more powerful motivator.

Let your child choose what to learn.

In school your child will be forced to work from an established curriculum, but at home she should be encouraged to pursue her personal areas of interest. If your child is obsessed with frogs, learn about frogs; if she wants to be a ballerina, allow her to dance and learn about ballet. Curiosity is a powerful motivator; use it to your advantage. In addition, both you and your child will become frustrated with one another if you try to force her to learn something that is of no interest to her; this will only make learning seem like a chore instead of a pleasure.

Freedom of choice is important to children in many settings. Allow your child to make as many choices as possible. Does she want the red shirt or the blue one? Does she want to paint or play outside? Choices are empowering, especially to a toddler striving to establish independence.

Use several different methods of teaching.

The brain encodes or stores information using several different filing systems. You can improve your child's ability to learn by using more than one of the five senses (hearing, seeing, feeling, smelling, and tasting). For example, we are more likely to remember a phone number when we say it aloud while we read it from a phone book, because we have both a visual and an auditory memory. (For more information on multiple mapping, see page 16.)

When we use different senses, we create multiple encoding, which increases the number of sites where the memory or information is stored. Add kinesthetic memory whenever possible by allowing your child to touch an object or to act out something instead of simply listening to or reading a message. For example, a hands-on learning experience at the aquarium might involve seeing a starfish, hearing about ocean life, smelling the salty water where the organism lives, and touching a starfish. Such a complete sensory experience helps children acquire knowledge even when their language centers are less developed than those of older children and adults.

Be a moving target.

You want to make learning as exciting as possible for your child. Your child will be aroused when new stimulation begins, but she will become bored if the stimulus continues without variation. (Think about how hard it is to focus on a person who speaks in a monotone.) Keep your child on her toes and you'll keep her interested in what you are saying. If it helps, don't be afraid to whisper, to shout (but not in anger), to clap, or to jump up and down. Just don't be boring.

Take a walk after your child learns something new.

Your child will learn more efficiently if you take a break after a teaching session. The neural connections formed by the brain when it learns new material need time for reinforcement before the brain must process more new information. If too much material is presented at one time, the brain does not have an opportunity to process all of it. Taking five minutes for a walk around the block or a brief trip to the playground should be a sufficient break. (Physical exercise works better than watching television or taking a bath because the release of epinephrine associated with exercise assists in the formation of the neural connections.)

Show your child how to do something, then get out of the way.

Your child may not know how to operate a toy or draw a circle when she sits down to try, but in many cases she can repeat your actions if you show her how. Demonstrate new skills to your child, then allow her to practice without interruption.

Help your child talk through an experience.

When working on a project, most adults talk to themselves or use inner language to solve a problem. Studies have shown that children also work better when they use inner language. You can help your child develop this skill by using words to describe what she is doing. "Let's get out the measuring cup and get a half cup of water. Look, there's the half-cup mark. Now, let's pour the water into the flour. . . ."

Help your child recognize patterns.

If you open your eyes you will notice thousands of patterns in the world around you, from the brickwork on the patio to the fabric in a shirt to the alternating colors of flowers in a garden. Help your child appreciate visual patterns by pointing them out to her; recognizing patterns will help her develop skills in mathematics.

Teach your child values.

It's your responsibility and privilege to provide a moral compass for your child. You need to talk about compassion, courage, honesty, fairness, and other characteristics you prize. Your child will use these values to shape her behavior throughout her life. Do your best to express—and to demonstrate through your actions—the morals you want to teach your child.

Let your child make noise and messes.
Learning and playing can be noisy and dirty business. Unless there is a good reason to keep things under control, allow your child to get rowdy every once in a while. Make siren noises, bark like a dog, or break out the finger paints on a sunny afternoon. Of course, you need to prevent your child from damaging property and you should work together to clean up the mess after you're finished playing, but during playtime don't be afraid to let your child be a child.

Think positive.
If you expect your child to learn and to behave well, she will often meet your expectations. Studies have shown that a positive attitude often leads to a positive result, perhaps because it shows your child that you have confidence in her ability to perform a given task.

Your can-do attitude helps your child build confidence in her abilities. Your child will work hard at a task if she believes that she can accomplish it. This expectation of success motivates children (as it does adults). The more confident your child feels, the harder she will try, the longer she will work, and the faster she will try again if she fails.

Don't confuse teaching confidence with boosting self-esteem. Self-confidence is about feeling competent and capable; self-esteem is about feeling good. To teach confidence, you need to allow your child to recognize her abilities and experience successes (then you can praise her). Every success helps raise both confidence and the chance of future successes. Allow your toddler to struggle and work hard at a task, whether it's getting dressed or putting crayons back in a box, so that she can learn to appreciate the rewards of hard work and concentrated effort. Whatever the challenge, encourage her on the sidelines and let her work through it on her own.

Allow your child to fail.

Your child needs to know that it's okay to try and to fail. Try to see your child's failures as opportunities for learning—and communicate the same message to her. If you harshly criticize your child when she fails, she will be afraid to accept challenges and to push herself. Instead of losing your temper over accidents and mistakes, teach your child how to clean up her own messes; if she spills her juice, teach her how to wipe it up. Accidents happen to all of us, but how we handle them is a matter of personal choice.

CHOOSING TOYS THAT ENCOURAGE GROWTH

Buy toys that require imagination rather than AA batteries.

Whenever possible, choose open-ended toys over those that do too much for the child. For example, avoid dolls that talk and crawl and those that come with an assigned set of interests ("this doll loves to ride her bike" or "this doll cares for animals"). Dolls like these don't leave enough to the imagination.

Instead, choose a more neutral toy that lets your child decide the outcome—what the doll says and how her voice sounds is up to your child; she decides whether the doll likes to ride its bike or not. While the gadgets and gimmicks that sell toys will appeal to a child in the short term, a toy that runs on a child's imagination will provide more hours of stimulating play in the long run.

Fill your child's toy box with active toys (jump ropes and balls), creative toys (paints and puppets), and educational toys (puzzles and board games). The age guides on most toy boxes should help you decide which toys are appropriate for your child's age and interests.

Introduce new toys one or two at a time.
Children love new toys, but too many choices can be overwhelming to an infant. Don't bombard your baby with lots of new things at one time; instead, slowly add new toys to her collection. Children are more likely to explore and play with new toys if they feel secure in their environment and have access to familiar objects.

Leave time for unstructured, imaginative play.
Make-believe is essential for intellectual growth. It gives a child the chance to role-play—"I'll be the mommy, you be the baby"—to test out her own ideas about the world, and to develop her creativity. Pretending to be a monster can help a child feel powerful and strong at a time when she feels particularly weak or threatened. Pretending to be angry with a doll can help a child resolve her feelings about a conflict with a parent. This role-playing helps the child experience the world from another person's point of view.

Research has shown that unstructured playtime helps children develop language and lengthens a child's attention span. While structured activities and computer games have a role in childhood, they should not take the place of old-fashioned games of let's pretend.

Watch television wisely.
It's up to you to establish an appropriate relationship between your child and television in the home. At its best, television can educate, inspire, and instruct. It has been found to be more effective than books or audiotapes for teaching children about dynamic processes, such as the growth of a flower or the formation of a rain cloud. No medium is better than television for showing physical demonstrations, such as putting together a puzzle or frosting a cake.

At its worst, television can promote violence, sexism, and commercialism; it can dull your child's natural curiosity and imagination and turn her into a passive spectator rather than an active participant in the events going on around her. Excessive television viewing has been linked to low test scores, decreased literacy, and poor physical health. In addition, studies have repeatedly shown a strict correlation between the amount of violence one observes on television and aggressive behavior, even in preschoolers.

To use television to your child's advantage, choose children's educational programming and limit the time she spends in front of the set to one hour or less per day. Children who sit and watch television for five or six hours a day are missing out on more valuable experiences.

Snuggle on the couch with your child and watch television together. You should be available to explain what is happening on the screen and to discuss the program with her. Ask your child questions like "What would you do if that happened to you? Why?" By discussing the program with her you can turn television into a learning experience.

Don't let your daily schedule revolve around television schedule. Use your VCR to tape appropriate programs of interest to your child and view them when it's convenient for you.

Use computers—if your child is interested.
Many experts believe that computers can enhance cognitive development in five- and six-year-olds (using appropriate software, of course), but they tend to be less convinced of its benefits for the three-and-under set.

If your little one has an interest in computers, let her experiment, but limit her computer time to fifteen to thirty minutes a day. During the years from birth to three, a child needs to devote most of her playtime to gross motor activities, such as running and jumping, and sensory-rich experiences, such as water play, painting, and drawing. Computer activities require fine motor skills and offer a relatively poor sensory experience.

Be sure to choose stimulating software. Avoid electronic worksheets that offer only rote learning experiences, and limit the use of glitzy video games that provide action but little learning. In general, open-ended software that allows for creative responses has more educational benefit than programs with fixed outcomes.

Don't think of the computer as an electronic baby-sitter; you will need to work with your child on the computer. Studies have shown that if an adult is present when the computer is on, children are more attentive, more interested, and less frustrated.

Which Toys and Activities Are Best?

1 to 3 months: High-contrast mobiles, unbreakable mirrors and activity centers attached to the crib, rattles, stuffed toys with black-and-white or brightly colored patterns, music boxes, recorded soft music, large colorful rings, books with high-contrast pictures

4 to 6 months: Beach balls; chunky bracelets; building blocks; squeaky toys; paper streamers; books made of cloth, vinyl, or cardboard; playing peekaboo with others

7 to 9 months: Stuffed animals, balls, nesting cylinders, pop-up toys, large dolls and puppets, bath toys, stacking toys, blocks, squeeze toys, playing patty-cake

10 to 12 months: Push-and-pull toys like miniature cars, ordinary household objects like empty egg cartons and large spoons, stacked rings on a spindle, cups and pails, bath toys, old magazines, playing simple ball games

13 to 15 months: Toy telephones, cups and clothespins, pushing a carriage or toy, acrobatics

16 to 18 months: Simple musical instruments, large colored beads, jack-in-the-boxes, blowing bubbles, playing in the sandbox

19 to 21 months: Rocking horses, toys to take apart and fit back together, small rubber balls, digging toys, large crayons, kiddie cars, water games, easy jigsaw puzzles, books with pictures of babies, shape sorters, pegboards, making mud pies, playing tag or hide-and-seek

22 to 24 months: Kiddie lawn mowers and kitchen sets for playing house; modeling clay; construction sets; action toys like trains, dump trucks, and fire engines; toy telephones, old magazines; baskets; tubes and containers with lids; dolls; outdoor toys and playground equipment

2 to 3 years: Beginner tricycles, mini-trampolines, roller skates or Rollerblades, dolls, and accessories like strollers and baby bottles, dress-up clothes, coloring books, crayons and markers, paints and easels, music, kiddie cassette players, swing sets, books, finger paints, mini–basketball hoops, woodworking benches, kiddie swimming pools.

ENCOURAGING YOUR CHILD'S ARTISTIC EXPRESSION

I used to draw like Raphael, but it has taken me a whole lifetime to learn to draw like a child.

—PABLO PICASSO,
twentieth-century Spanish painter and sculptor

Allow your child to experience art.
Nurture your child's natural instinct to draw, paint, sculpt, and express herself artistically. Art projects help children gain fine motor control as they learn to express themselves visually.

As soon as a child is able to pick up a crayon without putting it in her mouth (or at least without chewing on it all the time), she is ready to begin scribbling. Many babies and toddlers take great satisfaction in marking up a blank piece of paper. Between ages two and three, most children begin to express themselves through representational art (and sooner or later your child's giraffe will really look like a giraffe).

Pick up a paintbrush yourself.

Let your child see you express your creativity. If you act as though you are ashamed of your artistic ability or you make disparaging remarks about your work, your child may become self-critical as well and stop her artistic efforts.

Don't praise or judge your child's artwork.

Criticism and sometimes even praise can destroy a child's creativity. Once your child figures out that artwork is judged and compared with the works of others, she may feel that her work isn't as good and lose interest. Too much praise can sound insincere, especially when a child knows that a certain piece really isn't her finest work.

Instead of making remarks that could be interpreted as judgments, try to make observations about your child's work: "I like the way you used blue in that flower" or "That fish looks like it's ready to swim right off the page." These comments are precise and accurate, and they don't express favoritism for one work over another.

Keep plenty of art supplies on hand.

Stock your craft closet with markers, crayons, chalk, and paints. Give your child plenty of paper and lots of time to create her masterpieces. Set aside some of the projects and store them in a box or folder (your child will love seeing her early works when she is older).

Visit an art museum or gallery with your child.
These outings will give your child a chance to see the work of accomplished artists, to look at different artistic media, and to appreciate the importance that society puts on art.

Learning from Mistakes

Every child needs discipline. While positive reinforcement can encourage many behaviors, there are times when parents need to establish the boundaries and enforce the rules by punishing their children.

Studies have shown that how you handle discipline and decision making can either raise or lower your child's IQ. One study found that children living in hostile and restrictive homes experienced a decrease in IQ over a three-year period, while those growing up in loving and democratic homes experienced an 8-point jump in IQ.

You don't need to be a permissive parent or let your child run amok to boost her IQ. Instead, you need to take time to explain the rules to your child and to practice effective discipline. The following suggestions can help to make punishment an effective learning experience:

Explain the rules. It is essential that your child understand what is expected of her and why her behavior is unacceptable. This discussion will help your child learn to control her future behavior. When setting up the rules, explain the reasoning behind each rule, so that it will make sense to your child.

Catch your child in the act. Punishment is most effective when it is an immediate consequence of the misbehavior. The more time that passes between the misdeed and the punishment the greater the possibility your child will not understand why she is in trouble.

Be firm, but not harsh. A loud "No!" or "Stop that!" is more effective than a more mild-mannered voice when disciplining a child. Not surprisingly, studies have found that young children respond more to a strong reprimand (in the form of a loud buzzer) than they do to a milder warning. However, aggressive punishment is never warranted. Physical punishment or excessive verbal harshness creates high levels of anxiety that actually interfere with the child's ability to process the information, and the harshness can damage the relationship between the child and the disciplinarian. When you strike your child, you are showing her that you've lost control and that at times it's okay to use brute force to dominate another person. Your child will fearfully respond with better behavior, but she will also resent the behavior and model her conduct after yours.

Be consistent in handing out punishment. If a certain behavior goes unpunished sometimes and warrants a stiff penalty at other times, the punishment will be ineffective. In essence, you are rewarding your child each time she sneaks one over on you and avoids punishment. Inconsistent discipline can also confuse a small child, who gains a sense of security from being familiar with the rules.

When you want your child to do something, issue a command, don't ask a question. Asking "Would you please stop banging your hairbrush on the table?" gives your child an opportunity to say no. Instead, tell your child, "Please stop banging your hairbrush on the table." Make your instructions clear and authoritative. For the same reason, don't ask your child to do you a "favor"; your child needs to obey you without either one of you feeling the command is a request. Obedience is not optional.

Offer an incentive for compliance. If appropriate, give your child a good reason to obey. Rather than say, "Go get ready for bed," tell your child, "Go get ready for bed and I will tell you a story." Don't turn the situation into one of bribery, but give your child a good reason to want to comply with your instructions.

Make up after you punish. It is important that your child see you as a loving and affirming parent, not as a harsh disciplinarian. After you discipline your child, offer her some reassurance that you still love her and that everything is okay, even though her behavior is unacceptable.

Reinforce the positive. Punishing negative behavior is only half the battle. Make it a point to praise your child when she exhibits the behavior you want to see. You will get more of the behavior that you recognize and praise.

NEVER, NEVER shake your child. Each year, thousands of infants and toddlers suffer brain damage and death after being violently shaken. Children as old as five are vulnerable to shaken-baby syndrome, but infants between two and four months are at greatest risk. Approximately one out of every four shaken babies dies from the injuries. Those who survive may suffer blindness caused by bleeding around the brain and eyes or disabling brain damage, including mental retardation, paralysis, seizure disorders, and speech and learning disabilities. For information, call Childhelp USA (800-4-A-CHILD) or the Shaken Baby Syndrome Prevention Program (800-858-5222).

4 • Words to Grow On

Stimulating Speech and Language Development

Every child enters the world programmed to learn to communicate, first so that her needs can be met, then so that she can express her thoughts and ideas. Most parents anxiously await their child's first utterances, but few pause to reflect on the miraculous rate at which children acquire language skills. By the time your child reaches her first birthday, she understands a fair amount of what she hears and may be able to say a few simple words. By her second birthday, she understands much of what she hears and can express a range of ideas. By her third birthday, she can comprehend most of what she hears and she has a working vocabulary that can get her through most situations. In fact, by age three and a half, most children have a vocabulary of more than one thousand words.

Your child actually begins to learn language while still in the womb, where she hears her mother's voice and the sounds of the world around her. Researchers have found that babies as young as four days old can recognize their native tongue: French infants were found to nurse more vigorously when they heard French spoken than when exposed to Russian, and Russian infants preferred Russian to French.

At birth, babies continue to listen and to selectively mimic certain sounds. All of the world's six thousand languages use different sounds or phonemes to make up words. Sounds that babies do not hear as part of spoken language drop out of their vocabulary. In fact, by your child's first birthday, she has already started losing the ability to discriminate certain sounds that are not part of the language she hears on a regular basis. For example, American children lose the ability to make the click sound used in some African dialects, and Japanese children lose the ability to distinguish the difference between the *r* and *l* sounds because the *r* sound is not part of the Japanese language. However, Japanese Americans are exposed to both sounds on a regular basis, and they have no difficulty recognizing both sounds.

Children begin babbling and experimenting with phonemes during their first year. At about four to seven months of age, they begin cooing, or repeating vowel sounds, such as "aaaah" and "oooh." At seven to nine months old, they begin babbling, adding consonant sounds to the verbal gibberish. They eventually begin linking sounds with meanings, so that "mamama" and "da" become real words for "Mama" and "Dad." Once word recognition kicks in, children acquire language at an astounding rate. Experts estimate that at around eighteen months of age, children begin learning new words at the unfathomable rate of one every two hours.

This linguistic timetable seems to be biologically programmed. Deaf infants babble at the same age as hearing infants, indicating that children don't need to hear language to attempt to speak it. Deaf infants whose deaf parents communicate using sign language will babble and at the same time experiment with gestures and sign language in the way that a hearing infant would experiment with sounds.

However, for a child to move beyond babbling and to become fully verbal, she needs to hear language and to practice her skills. Many linguistic experts believe that there is a sensitive period for learning language, and that before puberty children can easily acquire one or more languages simultaneously and accurately.

Studies involving children who suffer brain damage show that the likelihood of regaining language skills depends on the age of the child when the accident occurs. Children who suffer brain damage before puberty usually recover most if not all of their language function without special therapy; children under age five show the best results. On the other hand, adolescents and adults who suffer the same injuries often require extensive therapy to regain a small portion of their language skills.

Two case studies further illustrate the importance of learning language before puberty. One case involved a child who was locked away in an isolated room in her home as an infant and not discovered by the authorities until she was fourteen years old. She overheard very little language and no one spoke directly to her. The other case involved a deaf woman whose family lived in isolation; she did not formally learn language until she was thirty-two years old. Both of these women were given extensive language training and both learned the meaning of many words, but neither was able to learn the rules of syntax and grammar that the typical child masters in childhood.

Word Watch

While every child learns to speak at a different rate, the following chart offers a general guide to typical language development.

AGE	AVERAGE NUMBER OF WORDS
12 months	3
18 months	22
2 years	272
3 years	896

AGE	LANGUAGE SKILLS
Birth to 2 months	Your child may begin cooing; she communicates by crying; she smiles at the sound of your voice; she may turn toward familiar sounds and voices; her hearing is fully mature.
3 months	Your child will try to make sounds after hearing others talk.
4 to 7 months	Your child begins making vowel sounds: "oooooh" and "eeeeeh."
5 to 7 months	Your child watches mouths carefully; she may try to imitate inflections and make new sounds by changing the shape of her mouth.

AGE	LANGUAGE SKILLS
7 to 9 months	Your child begins making consonant sounds: "ma" and "da."
9 months	Your child may respond to her name and recognize common words such as no.
9 to 12 months	Your child begins babbling; she may add gestures to words, such as waving bye-bye and shaking her head no; she may use exclamations, such as "Oh no!" and "Oh boy!"
12 months	Your child may say her first words; she shows much more control over intonation.
12 to 16 months	Your child enjoys rhymes and poetry; she gestures and uses props to communicate (brings a cup to indicate she wants something to drink).
14 to 16 months	Your child may follow simple directions, such as "Come here"; she may recognize the names of common words and body parts.
16 to 18 months	Your child enjoys pointing at words in books; no is her most common word; she may say her own name.

AGE	LANGUAGE SKILLS
18 to 20 months	Your child may make her first word combinations; she may ask the names of new objects: "What's that?"
18 to 24 months	Your child enjoys listening to stories and reading; she uses words to express emotions; she repeats words in conversation.
2 years	Your child may speak her first sentence; she imitates adult inflection in language.
2 to 3 years	Your child begins to use the pronouns I and me; she begins asking "Why?"; she learns to recognize the names of colors; she can follow more complicated stories in books; she can follow a two- or three-part command; she can recognize common objects and pictures; she uses four- or five-word sentences; strangers can understand her words.

TIPS FOR STIMULATING SPEECH

The way you communicate with your child can help her acquire language more efficiently. The following suggestions can help:

Talk to your child.

It's never too early to begin talking with your baby. Even if your little one doesn't know the difference between a diaper and a dandelion, the more you speak to your baby, the faster the auditory pathway in her brain will develop.

The more words a child hears, the faster she will develop a diverse vocabulary. Researchers at the University of Chicago found that infants whose mothers frequently spoke to them had a vocabulary of 131 more words than infants of less verbal mothers. At twenty-four months the difference increased to 295 words.

Look your child in the eye.

By maintaining close face-to-face contact you will be teaching your child about the gestures and facial expressions that reinforce verbal communication. It is especially important to use direct contact with babies and when giving instructions to older children.

You can watch your baby's movements to find out if she is listening. Researchers have found that infants move their arms to match the cadence of the speech they are hearing. These movements appear to help babies grasp the rhythm of language, and researchers suspect that they may encourage early verbal comprehension.

If your child diverts her eyes when you are talking to

her, stop, lift her chin gently with your finger, and say, "Look into my eyes." Resume talking when your child gazes up at you.

Don't be afraid to speak in parentese.

Psycholinguists use the term *parentese* to describe the high-pitched, singsong voice parents often use when talking to their babies. Babies do in fact respond better and pay more attention to short, simple sentences spoken in a high-pitched tone of voice, compared with the flatter, more monotonous tones used by most adults.

Allow one person to speak at a time.

For infants and toddlers the spoken word must compete with background noise and other stimulation for attention. If you're trying to talk to your child, minimize background noise, if possible. Also try to have only one person speak at a time so that your child can follow the conversation, even if she doesn't comprehend all of what she hears.

Talk about what your child is doing or experiencing.

When you feed, bathe, or lift your baby, describe what the child is experiencing. Talk about temperatures, smells, textures, and other sensory stimulation. Name and describe the objects of interest to your child. Label and name the common objects of your child's daily life, including body parts, household items, and toys.

Researchers analyzed the conversations between twenty-four mothers and their children at fifteen and twenty-one months of age. The amount of time the mothers spent talking about the objects their children were playing with affected the children's language development more than the amount and complexity of the mothers' speech. The children were highly motivated to learn the words for toys and objects that already interested them.

Tell your child a little bit more than what she asked for.
If your toddler says, "Doggie!" don't simply respond, "Yes, doggie." Give her more information: "Yes, that dog is called a Golden Retriever. It has long, golden hair." Your child may not pick up on all the details, but some of the new information will sink in.

Use correct pronunciation.
Your child will learn language more accurately and efficiently if you make an effort to correctly and clearly pronounce every word you speak. While baby words like "psghetti" and "mazagine" can be endearing, it's best to say "spaghetti" and "magazine" so that your child can learn to correct her mistakes. It is also important to hire caretakers who pronounce words clearly and accurately.

Use correct grammar.
The critical period for acquiring grammar occurs before age three. Your child will model her language structure after the patterns she hears during her daily life, so always use grammatically correct speech. If your child is in daycare, be sure that the caretakers are good grammatical role models.

Gently correct your little one's verbal mistakes.
Rather than harshly pointing out a child's grammatical or pronunciation errors, you can offer a subtle but effective

correction as part of the conversation. For example, if your child says, "I heared Daddy come," you can respond by recasting the sentence: "Yes, you heard Daddy come home." Over time, your child will mimic the new grammatical form and correct the mistake. Studies have found that children whose parents recast or expand their speech tend to pick up on grammatical and syntactical principles earlier than other children do. In addition, they tend to score higher on standardized tests of expressive language ability.

Have conversations with your baby.

Your baby may not use words, but she can participate in the mutual give-and-take of conversation. Take turns when talking or interacting with your baby. Exchanging smiles or words and gibberish is a first step, but it is important for your baby to learn the basic structure of conversation. By seven or eight months of age, most children will sit silently while someone else talks to them, waiting until the speaker is finished before they speak (or vocalize). This golden rule of conversation—don't speak while someone else is talking—appears to be learned quite early.

Children who converse with their parents frequently and ask them questions tend to learn grammar more readily, have larger-than-average vocabularies, and score higher on academic achievement tests than less talkative children. In addition, your child needs to understand the rules of conversation in order to get along socially. Many maladjusted children simply can't comprehend how to take another person's point of view into consideration when deciding how to behave. All too often, these children don't understand why they can't get along with their peers.

One way to reinforce the idea of taking turns is to play games like peekaboo that involve waiting for the other person to respond. Introduce this game, as well as other give-and-take exchanges, when your baby is four to six months old.

Don't put words into your child's mouth.
Sometimes toddlers need a few moments to come up with the right word when they're trying to express an idea. Don't jump in and tell your child what you think she is trying to say (even if you're certain you know what word she is searching for). Your child will learn faster and develop more confidence in her ability to speak for herself if she is not interrupted when it is her turn to speak.

Play the preposition game.
By the time your child reaches age two, teach her the correct use of prepositions (under, over, inside, etc.), articles (a, an, the), and connectives (and, but, or, etc.). To help your child grasp the concept of object placement, turn an object over, then put it under, over, outside, and inside something else.

Give your child paper, markers, and crayons.
Toddlers readily grasp the idea that writing is an important adult activity. By age one, many children begin scribbling in an attempt to mimic grown-up writing. While you may discount this early writing as nothing more than a waste of paper, it is actually evidence of burgeoning linguistic aware-

ness. It allows preschoolers to make the connection between writing and reading, between gestures put down on paper and the written word.

Watch out for ear infections.

Children who have chronic or recurring ear infections before age four may experience temporary hearing loss, which can cause problems with the development of language and reading skills. These children may not be able to discriminate between certain sounds, such as "ch" and "sh," without speech therapy.

If your child suffers from chronic ear infections, watch for signs of hearing loss. Discuss the matter with your pediatrician, who should be able to perform a hearing test or refer you to a pediatric audiologist, if necessary.

STRATEGIES TO PROMOTE READING

Read to your child every day.

Many studies have found that children who are early readers come from families where parents read to their children, often from the time they are infants. Try to choose a regular time each day (such as before bedtime or after lunch), and read to your child for fifteen minutes or so. Begin reading regularly at six to nine months of age; your child will probably understand more than you expect, and even if she doesn't she will enjoy snuggling close to you and looking at the pictures.

When you read to your child she picks up subtle but important facts about the skill, such as reading from left to right and turning pages. As your child hears the written word, she will learn to recognize the rhythm of language and the flow of words. She will cultivate an ear for language, which can help her to learn to read and write. Despite these many benefits, only about half of all infants and toddlers are read to by their parents on a regular basis.

Make learning to read fun.
When your child is ready to begin to decode the written word, choose books that capture her attention and stimulate her senses. Explore anything that makes the book enjoyable to your child, including pop-up cutouts, unique illustrations, and computerized sound effects.

Read poetry to your child.
Many toddlers love nursery rhymes and Dr. Seuss because they like to experience the rhyme and rhythm in language. Many traditional nursery rhymes make little sense to children (and some make little sense to adults), so add some contemporary poetry that includes imagery your child can appreciate.

Let your child catch you reading.
Say what you will about the importance of reading, if you don't read in your home, your child will pick up on the fact that you don't value reading. Read for your own pleasure. Subscribe to newspapers and magazines; check out a good book from the library. Your child will be more impressed by your example than by your claims that reading is important.

"What was that about?"
After reading a story, ask your child a couple of questions in an attempt to encourage comprehension and analysis:

"What was important in the story?" "How would you feel if you were the main character in the story?"

CHILDREN AND SECOND LANGUAGES

Because of the way the brain acquires language, your child can learn a second or third language almost effortlessly during the first three years of life. In addition, your child will speak each language without a foreign accent, as long as the person teaching your child uses correct pronunciation.

During infancy and the toddler years, a child's brain stores neurological information about the sounds she hears associated with speech. These bits of language information become the building blocks of all future speech and vocabulary.

A child can store language information for one, two, or more languages, though children learning more than one language at a time may show some slight delays in vocabulary development. Once a child has developed the neural circuitry for a foreign language, she can use this information to expand her vocabulary and master it.

The catch is that the brain becomes less adept at storing language information later in childhood. If your child were to wait until age ten or twelve (or later) to begin studying a new language, she would be forced to use the sounds she had already stored in her brain to learn the new language. This is why most people who try to learn a foreign language after early puberty cannot speak without a foreign accent, no matter how much they practice.

Evidence also suggests that children who learn a second

language in early childhood experience direct language learning, which means that they do not have to go through the mental process of translation in order to switch from one language to another. An older child or adult who learns a new language must translate from one tongue to the other. Children who are taught in English to speak Spanish must go through the translation process. However, young children taught by someone who speaks only the second language to them learn through the direct, or mother's, method, and they store the language in their brains without the need for translation.

If you would like your child to learn a second language, it makes sense to begin instruction as early as possible, certainly before age twelve. Since your child will mirror the speech patterns of her teacher, choose someone who speaks the foreign language with generally accepted pronunciation.

Red Flags: Warning Signs of Developmental Problems

Poor articulation or pronunciation is the most common language problem among children. Does your child seem to be behind her peers in repeating certain sounds? Is her speech unintelligible to people outside the immediate family at age three? If so, discuss the matter with your pediatrician, who can rule out any physical problems for the speech impairment, and then contact a speech therapist for professional assistance. Most problems involving articulation can be corrected with therapy; resolving them early can prevent difficulties once your child is ready to start school.

Keep your ears open for other signs of delayed speech. If your child is slow to develop the following skills, make an appointment with her pediatrician for a complete hearing and language evaluation.

BIRTH TO 3 MONTHS
- Your child does not turn toward you when you speak to her.

4 TO 6 MONTHS
- Your child does not turn or respond to noises, such as doorbells, barking dogs, or someone calling her name.

- Your child does not coo or make vowel-based noises.

7 TO 9 MONTHS
- Your child does not turn when you call her name.

9 MONTHS TO 1 YEAR
- Your child does not attempt to imitate speech sounds.

- Your child does not babble using consonant sounds.

1 TO 2 YEARS
- Your child cannot point to pictures in a book if you name the object.

- Your child does not recognize words for common items, such as "ball" or "bottle."

- Your child does not seem to understand simple questions, such as "Where is your blanket?"

2 TO 3 YEARS

- Your child does not understand the use of common prepositions, such as "up" and "down."

- Your child does not combine two or three words at a time.

- Your child cannot name common household objects.

- Your child cannot follow a two-part command, such as "Please get your ball and bring it to me" or "Pick up your blanket and put it on the bed."

3 TO 4 YEARS

- Your child cannot answer simple questions.

- Your child cannot be clearly understood by people outside the immediate family.

- Your child cannot speak in four-word sentences.

- Your child cannot pronounce the sounds of the English language correctly, including all the consonant sounds and the common consonant blends.

5 · Me, Myself, and I

Building Emotional Health and Personal Identity

For your child, the first three years of life will offer the best and the worst of times. In early childhood, most children experience periods of unparalleled bliss and security, when the world feels safe and loving and there is nothing to fear. But they also must endure unpredictable times of fear and despair, when the world feels cold and lonely and frightening in ways that most adults rarely experience.

Your role as a parent will never be more important to your child's emotional development than it is during the early years of childhood. The way you interact with your child in the first two to three years of life will shape her expectations of the world and her attitudes toward life. The noted psychologist Erik Erikson has argued that a child who is loved and nurtured will learn to trust her environment and to be open to new experiences and opportunities for learning. (Most experts in the field agree with his assessment.) As the child matures, she will develop a healthy and secure personal identity.

On the other hand, according to Erikson, a child whose needs are not consistently met or who is treated harshly will not learn to trust that the world is a safe place. In turn, she will experience feelings of guilt, shame, and inferiority that can last a lifetime.

Not surprisingly, a child's intellectual growth can be impaired by emotional problems and the failure to develop personal autonomy. Children simply cannot live up to their full potential if they do not develop a healthy personal identity. The following suggestions can help you nurture your child as you encourage her to build a healthy self-image.

Make every effort to snuggle your baby and to form a healthy attachment.

Early bonding between a baby and her parents can set the stage for the healthy development of trust in the outside world. Babies who form secure attachments achieve more intellectually and developmentally than infants who do not form positive attachments. Studies have found that babies who were securely bonded at twelve to eighteen months of age were social leaders, better problem solvers at age two, more creative in their play, and more popular with other children as playmates, compared with children who did not experience secure attachments with their caregivers. Toddlers with insecure attachments were hesitant to play with other children, socially withdrawn, less willing to explore and to learn about their environment, and generally less assertive.

Some parents talk about falling in love and bonding with their babies when they first see their infants in the moments after birth, but the truth is that secure emotional attachments evolve over time. In essence, the process involves both the parent and the child learning to read the other's signals and to respond to the other's needs. The parent learns how to interpret the baby's cries and movements, while the infant learns how to communicate her needs in a way that elicits an appropriate response from her parents.

Human beings are biologically programmed to form parent-child attachments, but the process takes some effort. One of the easiest and most effective ways of encouraging bonding and attachment is to have close physical contact with your child by snuggling. Research has shown that the more close contact a mother has with her child, the better she can respond to her baby's needs and the more secure the child feels in response.

As part of a research project, mothers were assigned to one of two groups—one group received a soft, pouchlike baby carrier (the close-contact group) and a second received a plastic infant seat (the control group). Three and a half months later, the mothers in the close-contact group were significantly more responsive to their babies' cries than mothers in the control group. At thirteen months, the babies in the close-contact group were much more likely to be securely attached to their mothers.

Make every effort to meet your baby's needs.
Your baby is completely dependent on you to understand her needs and to satisfy them. A newborn has limited ways to communicate with you; she can cry, squirm, and make strange faces, but ultimately it's up to you to interpret these signals. Anyone can learn to decipher a baby's needs if she

spends enough time as a caregiver, though there may be a long period of trial and error as the caregiver learns how to read the child's signals.

When a child finds that her needs are consistently and lovingly met, she begins to trust that someone will come to her aid when she is in distress. To the child, the world is a secure, safe, and comfortable place, where cries of hunger are met with food, cries of fear are met with comfort, and cries of boredom are met with a warm smile.

If, on the other hand, you refuse to respond to your child's cries, you are teaching her to feel helpless and alone. When children do not form emotional bonds with their caregivers, they cannot thrive emotionally, intellectually, or physically. In fact, studies of orphaned infants done during World War II found that babies who did not experience a secure emotional bond often stopped eating; many became seriously ill and some died.

It is impossible to spoil a child by meeting her basic needs. It is impossible to provide too much security or too much comfort to an infant. Remember, as a parent, your goal is to teach your child that she is accepted and loved.

Strive to provide a consistent caretaker and predictable environment for your child.
Your child needs to be comfortable and familiar with the people who take care of her. Daycare and baby-sitting arrangements that frequently change can be confusing and frightening for a small child. Once a child has learned to trust a caregiver, an abrupt change can be quite disconcerting and can create feelings of insecurity and instability.

Since more than half of all mothers work outside the

home at least part-time, child care is an important issue for millions of American families. According to the U.S. Department of Labor, 25 percent of infants and toddlers are cared for exclusively by their parents, 27 percent are cared for by other relatives, 7 percent stay home with a sitter, 25 percent stay in daycare homes, and 16 percent are cared for in large daycare facilities.

While there is considerable controversy about which type of arrangement is best for a child's emotional and intellectual development, most studies show that a child is not at risk of emotional insecurity if she receives excellent care from qualified professionals. The catch, of course, is that the quality of daycare in the United States is highly variable.

If you must leave your child to go to work, take pains to find excellent care. Look for a good child-to-caregiver ratio (no more than three infants, four toddlers, or eight preschoolers per adult) and low staff turnover. The caregivers should be warm, affirming, interested in the children, and responsive to the children's needs. The facility should be equipped with age-appropriate toys and games.

Minimize the stress level in your household.
While many harried parents will consider this easier said than done, it is essential to try to make your child feel relaxed and safe at home. During times of stress, your child's body secretes the hormone cortisol. In low to moderate amounts, cortisol is harmless, but when it is present at high levels day in and day out, it will kill brain cells and impair your child's intellectual development.

Cortisol can actually interfere with the brain's ability to

form memory, which is essential for learning. The hormone inhibits the use of blood sugar by the hippocampus, the part of the brain that helps to store memories. Without enough blood sugar for energy, the brain experiences short-term memory difficulty, which is why people under stress may not be able to remember the events that happen to them.

The stress hormones also interfere with concentration. Cortisol blocks the functioning of the brain's neurotransmitters, making it difficult both to access memories that have already been stored and to make appropriate connections within the brain.

Chronically stressed or traumatized children actually exhibit changes in their brain size. The area of the brain that is responsible for emotions and positive attachments tends to be 20 to 30 percent smaller in abused children than in children raised in normal environments.

Children who experience high levels of stress in their first three years of life tend to remain highly sensitive to it. The neural circuitry in their brains has left them hard-wired to respond—and often overreact—to the slightest suggestion of fear or danger. Researchers have found that abused children actually exhibit greater activity in the region of the brain known as the locus coeruleus, which monitors arousal. Many of these children with overzealous stress sensors tend to be hyperactive, anxious, and often impulsive.

Spend time with your child.
Many adults feel overwhelmed by the demands of their daily lives and don't spend much relaxed time enjoying

their children. Often these harried parents create harried children who are involved in many extracurricular activities and programs. These fast-track children often suffer from stress, overburdened by excessive expectations.

Often, the simple, unscheduled times a family spends together make the biggest difference in a child's development. For example, one interesting study focused on characteristics of children who earned high scores on the Scholastic Aptitude Tests (SATs). The researchers found one unexpected factor that was more important than IQ, social circumstances, or economic status. Children who did well on the test all ate dinner with their parents and families on a regular basis. Clearly, adult conversation and parental involvement can enhance a child's intellectual development.

Speak lovingly to your child.

Your child will believe what you say, whether the message you send is "You are a great kid" or "You can't do anything right." Children under age three instinctively accept what they are told by authority figures without question.

Because children internalize messages so readily, they learn very easily. The material they are told enters the subconscious mind and lodges there. As a result, children who receive positive messages form a positive self-image and those who receive damaging or destructive messages form a negative self-image.

You can literally shape your child's self-image during the first few years of her life by conveying affirming and loving messages. This is a powerful responsibility, one that parents should not take lightly. Do not make damaging remarks, no matter how frustrating your child's behavior may be, since she will hear and remember the words you say, even if you don't really mean them. In addition, make an effort to offer positive messages that will build up your child's self-image. You can't tell a child too often that she is special, that she is capable, and that she is loved.

Encourage your child to talk about feelings and emotions. Between the ages of one and two, most children begin to learn words to express emotions such as happiness, anger, or sadness. The more time you spend helping your child understand her feelings by discussing them, the more understanding and empathetic your child will be. In fact, one study found that three-year-olds who talked about their emotions were much better at interpreting the emotions of others three years later. These empathetic children also tended to experience good relationships with their friends and classmates.

Let your actions demonstrate your concern for others. You are the most important role model for your child. If you want your child to grow up to exhibit positive social behavior, you need to live a socially responsible life. In other words, don't just talk about charity and good deeds, practice them. Studies have found that children who observe charitable and helpful behavior tend to model their own behavior in the same way. Researchers have also found that adults who are unusually generous and charitable tend to have had positive and affirming relationships with their parents, who were also concerned about helping others.

While many public broadcasting networks tend to offer children's programming with prosocial themes, these lessons are not particularly effective unless an adult watches the program and encourages or reinforces the importance of the social lesson. You can't rely on a daily dose of *Sesame Street* to teach your child to share, cooperate, and show concern for others.

Teach your child self-control.

One of the biggest challenges facing children between their second and third birthdays is the struggle to learn self-control. If you have spent much time with two-year-olds, you know that they can be incredibly defiant and uncooperative as they attempt to exert their will, often with a loud and unrelenting "NO!" While this developmental phase can be exasperating for parents, it is essential for healthy emotional development.

How you as a parent respond to your child will help determine her attitude toward authority figures and her ability to exhibit self-control. Parents who respond to a two-year-old's outbursts by criticizing, threatening, or physically intervening in the situation tend to cultivate defiance in the child. Parents who respond with a clear and concise "No," followed by a calm explanation of why the child can't have her way in the given situation, help the child understand why she can't always get her way. In most cases, this more rational approach will eventually yield compliance— and it will help your child develop a healthy attitude toward authority figures.

Teach your toddler to clean her room.

Young children thrive on repetition and order. Between the ages of two and a half and three and a half, most toddlers insist on routine. This behavior may represent your child's attempt to develop a sense of order and continuity in her world from which she can draw valid and workable ideas about how the world works. You can use this built-in instinct to teach your little one to maintain an orderly existence—and a clean room.

Store your child's toys on low, open shelves so that she can reach them and independently choose what to use. While most children will pull out all the toys and dump them on the floor, you can teach your child to play with toys one at a time and to put them away after using them. Use color tape to identify toys and their proper locations, so that your child can accurately return items to the appropriate place.

If you allow your child to grow up without teaching her good habits of orderliness and cleanliness, you may spend the next few decades cleaning up after her and nagging her to pick up her messes. You will also be shortchanging your child if you clean up after her, because she won't get the feeling of accomplishment and satisfaction that come from doing it herself.

Nightmares and Night Terrors

While we all have bad dreams from time to time, many children experience nightmares on a regular basis, starting at around age three. Your child's world can be confusing and at times disturbing. Her subconscious may attempt to work through these feelings in her dreams.

A night terror is a different type of sleep problem that usually occurs in children between the ages of six months and four years. During these episodes, your child may open her eyes wide, scream, and toss in bed, often without waking. Your child may appear to be in the throes of a nightmare, but her brain wave patterns show that she is in the deepest levels of sleep. In fact, she is unconscious, even if she moves and her eyes open. In most cases, she won't remember the episode in the morning.

Experts believe night terrors are caused by developmental overload of the child's nervous system. It is not a symptom of an emotional or psychological problem, but you should mention the episode to your child's pediatrician.

In handling nightmares, don't tell your child that her dream is not real. Instead, reassure your child that she is safe and sound. Don't play games with your child to make the object of fear disappear. If you acknowledge the monster under the bed by chasing it away, you validate your child's fear. Here's a better way: show your child that there is nothing under the bed right now. (This does not negate your child's experience or emotions, but it does provide reassurance about her current security. In other words, you aren't telling her there never was a monster under the bed, you're simply showing her that there isn't one there now.)

MILESTONES IN EMOTIONAL DEVELOPMENT

Your child is like no other. Her smile, the way she yawns, and how she reacts to the world are all completely her own. It is difficult to define what "normal" emotions are for children three and under. The following table provides some basic behaviors and expressions of emotions common in children at certain ages:

Birth to 3 months
- Your child is alert to loud sounds and bright lights. She quiets and becomes calm when held and snuggled.

- Your child will recognize your voice and turn to make eye contact.

- Your child cries when in pain, stressed, or in need of attention.

- Your child begins to develop a social smile.

- Your child enjoys being with other people.

- Your child imitates movements and facial expressions.

3 to 8 months
- Your child learns to smile and becomes increasingly affectionate and demonstrative toward her parents.

- Your child learns to recognize certain people; she may cry when her mother or caregiver leaves the room.

- Your child laughs when playing to express pleasure.

- Your child exhibits curiosity when inspecting new toys; her moods change quickly.

- Your child begins to learn to calm herself in certain situations.

- By the fifth month, your child may become more assertive in reaching for toys. She expresses anger when someone takes away something she wants.

- By the sixth month, stranger anxiety may begin. In most cases, your child responds well to other children.

- At seven months, your child may offer hugs and kisses. She may raise her arms to be picked up.

- At eight months, your child may begin to complain when confined in a crib or playpen.

- Your child may be interested in her mirror image.

- Your child may enjoy social play.

8 to 16 months

- Your baby may begin to model her moods and behavior after those around her. For example, if she hears another child cry, she may begin to cry as well.

- Your child may show signs of jealousy or sibling rivalry.

- Your child may become attached to a blanket, teddy bear, or other object that offers security.

- Your child may test her environment more, seeking pleasurable experiences.

- Your child becomes better able to control her anger and dissatisfaction.

- Your child begins to develop distinct types of interactions with people; she interacts in a different way with parents, siblings, friends, and strangers.

- Your child may be anxious or shy with strangers.

- Your child may cry when a parent leaves the room.

- Your child may show a preference for certain people or toys.

- Your child may extend her arms and legs to help get dressed.

16 to 24 months

- Your child may become more demanding of your time and attention.

- Your child begins to exhibit more obvious signs of her personality.

- Your child will begin to communicate feelings with a more explicit intent.

- Your child may flail her arms or run away to communicate no. She may even hit her parents in anger.

- Your child may respond to your requests. If reprimanded, your child will cry; if praised, she will show pleasure. She becomes more sophisticated at reading the emotional needs of other people, particularly her parents.

- Your child may go off by herself when emotionally confused or upset.

- By eighteen months, your child may express frustration by having temper tantrums.

- Your child is probably not very good at sharing.

- Your child may obey simple rules if praised adequately.

- Your child may show signs of fear of thunder, lightning, large animals, and the dark.

- Your child may begin to sympathize with other people.

- By twenty-two months, your child may begin to cooperate with others. She may begin to play well with other children, though children of that age tend to engage in parallel play (each child plays on her own but enjoys the other's company).

- Your child expresses frustration with new activities.

- By age two, your child may become manipulative and bossy.

- Your child may demonstrate independence by playing or doing things on her own.

- Your child may begin to show signs of defiant behavior.

- Your child's separation anxiety may increase at eighteen months, then fade by age two.

2 to 3 years
- Your child sees the world through the lens of what she wants and needs.

- Your child has frequent mood swings. She may pout when scolded. She can express sadness.

- Your child may enjoy playing with other children in play groups.

- Your child begins to recognize which behaviors are acceptable and which are not.

- Your child may not be able to concentrate on new tasks for more than a few minutes.

- Your child may show a greater level of sympathy or concern for family members and friends.

- Your child will learn to throw temper tantrums and to recover from them.

- Your child may test certain behaviors to gauge the reactions of others.

- Your child may experience more pleasure—and possibly anxiety—due to her imaginative play.

- Your child is able to express more of her feelings using words.

- Your child may worry more about distressing events.

- Your child may seek repeated reassurance about her well-being and family.

- Your child understands "mine" and "yours."

- Your child can take turns in a game.

- Your child shows spontaneous affection to familiar playmates and family members.

- Your child may initiate discussions about emotional issues.

Red Flags: Warning Signs of Emotional Problems

Children can experience a range of emotional problems. Some issues can be resolved with additional parental attention, but others may require professional assistance. If your child exhibits the following behavioral or emotional problems, discuss the matter with your pediatrician or a pediatric psychologist.

BIRTH TO 6 MONTHS
- Your child fails to gain weight or develop physically within "normal" ranges.

- Your child has little appetite.

- Your child does not seem interested in eye contact or human interaction.

- Your child seems ultrasensitive to sounds.

- Your child has tic-like jerks or spasms of the face or limbs.

6 TO 12 MONTHS
- Your child exhibits behaviors that prove to be self-injurious.

- Your child does not have regular sleeping and eating patterns.

- Your child does not imitate sounds or attempt language.

- Your child does not exhibit appropriate emotional responses to fear or pleasure.

- Your child seems apathetic or disinterested in things going on around her.

- Your child is excessively fearful of strangers.

- Your child exhibits ongoing developmental delays.

1 TO 2 YEARS

- Your child is withdrawn and lonely.

- Your child is excessively distracted.

- Your child is aggressive or irritable and is difficult to calm.

- Your child sleepwalks or wanders around in the night.

2 TO 3 YEARS

- Your child is excessively fearful.

- Your child does not talk.

- Your child cannot focus on a given task for ten minutes or longer.

- Your child experiences ongoing and excessive sibling rivalry.

- Your child exhibits hyperactive behavior.

- Your child experiences extreme separation anxiety.

- Your child is excessively aggressive and is slow to recover from angry outbursts.

6·Turning On the Motor

Encouraging Movement and Motor Development

Most parents have paradoxical feelings about their children: they want to savor the precious moments of childhood, but at the same time they want to push their children toward developmental landmarks as an outward sign of the physical superiority of their offspring. "She's been walking since she was nine months old" and other claims of advanced development can be a source of great pride for some parents.

In reality, you can't force your baby to grow up faster than nature intends. The body has its own developmental timetable based on brain and neurological development. (See the discussion of myelinization in chapter 1, on pages 11 to 12.) Your healthy child will crawl and walk and run—but not until her brain and body are ready for the task.

If you expect too much from your little one, both you and your child will feel frustrated and anxious. Parenting involves plenty of struggles without creating new ones. Unless your child has a health problem (in which case she needs to be under a doctor's care), she will reach all of the developmental milestones, though perhaps not at the pace you would choose.

While you should not set unrealistic expectations for your child's development, it is healthy for you to encourage her sensory and motor development. The following suggestions can help you provide opportunities for growth.

Give your baby plenty of tummy time.

Your baby will develop motor skills from the head downward. Your child's first challenge will be to strengthen her neck and shoulders to gain head control. When placed on her abdomen, she will learn to lift and turn her head, to rise up on her shoulders, to rotate her upper body, and eventually to roll over. This is no small feat, and it will require tremendous effort on the part of your child.

Make sure your baby spends at least fifteen minutes playing on her abdomen every day. (NOTE: Pediatricians recommend that parents avoid putting their children to sleep on their tummies, so do not allow your infant to fall asleep in this position.)

Touch, caress, and massage your baby.

Evidence suggests that stroking your baby—from her head toward her toes and from the center of her body out to her extremities—soothes her and stimulates the pathways of neuromuscular development and nerve cell insulation.

When stroking your child be aware that light touch can tickle and feel annoying rather than calming. Instead, use a firm but gentle touch or, better yet, experiment with different techniques so that you can discover what type of approach seems to work best for your child.

Infants also thrive on skin-to-skin contact, which provides warmth as well as the comforting scent of a loving parent. Snuggle with your baby as soon as you can after birth, and continue to do so as frequently as is practical during infancy. It will strengthen the parent-child bond and enhance neurological development.

In one study, researchers looked at the development of 120 babies who were given one hour and forty minutes of skin-to-skin stroking during the first three days of life. The stimulated babies gained weight faster and mastered certain stages of motor development more rapidly than the babies who did not receive the additional touching.

Expose your child to the world of touch.
You can stimulate your child's sense of touch by providing a rich and varied tactile environment. One of the easiest sources of stimulation are swatches of different fabrics, such as corduroy, fake fur, velvet, vinyl, wool, satin, nylon, and cotton. Allow your child to touch them one at a time, while you name the sensation: "This is soft," "This is smooth," "This is scratchy."

Take time to play with your child.
Playtime activities can help to stimulate your child's physical development. For example, a toddler can strengthen motor skills by climbing stairs while holding your hand, kicking balls, navigating obstacle courses, and playing games like Follow the Leader. A two-year-old may be ready to tackle developmental challenges like pedaling a tricycle, throwing a ball, standing on one leg, or playing a simple game of Simon Says.

MILESTONES IN MOTOR DEVELOPMENT

The general guide to average motor development that follows should not be considered a blueprint for every child's development. If you are concerned about your child's motor development, discuss the matter with her pediatrician.

1 month

GROSS MOTOR

- Your child makes jerky, quivering movements that will become smoother as her nervous system matures and her muscle control improves.

- Most of your child's actions are reflexive, such as sucking and bringing closed fists up to her mouth.

- Your child thrusts her arms and legs.

- Your child's head flops backward if unsupported.

- Your child keeps her hands in fists most of the time.

FINE MOTOR

- Your child is not capable of fine motor activity at this age.

VISUAL

- Your child can focus eight to twelve inches away.

- Your child's eyes wander and sometimes cross.

- Your child prefers human faces to other patterns.

2 months

GROSS MOTOR

- Your child's legs start to straighten from the inward-curving newborn position.

- Your child struggles to raise her head.

- Some of your child's reflexes begin to fade near month's end.

FINE MOTOR

- Your child opens and closes her hands carefully.

- Your child may hold an object for a few moments at a time.

- Your child may bring her hands to her mouth.

VISUAL

- Your child watches faces very carefully.

- Your child follows moving objects with her eyes.

3 months

GROSS MOTOR

- Your child pushes down on her legs when held in a standing position on a firm surface.

- Your child learns to bounce.

- Your child may raise her head and chest when lying on her stomach.

- Your child's kicks gain force as her hips and knee joints become more flexible.

- Your child can support her upper body with her arms when lying on her stomach.

- Your child can stretch her legs and kick when on her stomach or back.

FINE MOTOR

- Your child may swipe at dangling objects.

- Your child should be able to move both arms equally well when lying on her back.

VISUAL

- Your child recognizes familiar people at a distance.

- Your child uses her hands and eyes together.

4 months

GROSS MOTOR

- Your child may learn how to shift her weight from side to side and flip over.

- Your child's upper body and arms strengthen; she may sit up with support.

- Your child often leans for balance.

FINE MOTOR

- Your child reaches with her arms.

- Your child can hold a rattle and put it in her mouth.

5 months

GROSS MOTOR

- Your child has better physical control of her trunk, head, and neck.

- Your child can raise her head and hold it up while lying on her stomach.

- Your child grabs her feet and brings them to her mouth when resting on her back.

FINE MOTOR

- Your child may switch or transfer an object from one hand to the other.

- Your child may be able to hold her bottle.

- Your child uses a raking grasp rather than a pincer grasp (using the thumb and index finger).

6 months

GROSS MOTOR

- Your child can roll over in both directions.

- Your child can maintain balance while sitting because she has stronger abdominal and back muscles.

- Your child may be able to move forward on her stomach, pushing with her legs.

FINE MOTOR

- Your child may reach out for objects while sitting.

VISUAL

- Your child has full color vision.

- Your child is better able to track moving objects with her eyes.

7 *months*

GROSS MOTOR

- Your child can support her entire weight on her legs.

- Your child pivots when sitting to reach objects.

- Your child may get into a sitting position by pushing up on her arms.

FINE MOTOR

- Your child can clasp hands; she enjoys banging objects together.

- Your child may grab for a toy with one hand.

VISUAL

- Your child's distance vision (across the room) improves.

8 *months*

GROSS MOTOR

- Your child's coordination improves.

- Your child may begin to crawl, often pushing backward at first.

- Your child may scoot across the room on her bottom instead of crawling.

FINE MOTOR

- Your child can let go of objects voluntarily.

- Your child has learned to open her fingers at will; she can drop and throw objects.

- Your child may be able to use a pincer grasp.

9 months

GROSS MOTOR

- Your child may begin to pull up on furniture and stand.

- Your child may learn how to bend her knees and sit down after standing.

FINE MOTOR

- Your baby can put objects in a container and then take them out.

- Your baby may finger holes on a Peg-Board; she enjoys toys with moving parts like wheels or levers.

10 months

GROSS MOTOR

- Your child may walk while holding on to furniture; she may let go momentarily and stand without support.

- Your child can sit confidently.

FINE MOTOR

- Your child may hold a crayon and try to scribble.

- Your child is intrigued by tiny things.

11 months

GROSS MOTOR

- Your child strengthens the skills she acquired in previous months.

FINE MOTOR

- Your child likes to turn pages, but rarely one by one.

- Your child is fascinated by hinges and may swing doors back and forth.

12 months

GROSS MOTOR

- Your child may take her first independent steps. (Half of all children walk at about their first birthday.) Her first steps will be shaky, of course. Expect lots of stumbles and falls.

13 months

GROSS MOTOR

- Your child may walk with her feet wide apart, toes pointing out.

- Your child may use her arms for balance when walking.

FINE MOTOR

- Your child may point with her index finger.

- Your child can accurately pick up small objects with her thumb and index finger (the pincer grasp).

14 months

GROSS MOTOR

- Your child may stoop to pick up a toy and carry it across the room.

FINE MOTOR

- Your child can hold two or three objects in one hand.

- Your child likes to turn containers over to dump out the contents.

15 months

GROSS MOTOR

- Your child can climb stairs on her hands and knees; she descends by crawling and sliding.

- Your child can push or pull a toy while walking.

FINE MOTOR

- Your child builds small towers of blocks and then knocks them down.

16 months

GROSS MOTOR

- Your child may try to kick a ball but steps on it instead.

- Your child can walk sideways and backwards.

- Your child quickens her pace when excited or being chased.

- Your child can carry several toys while walking.

FINE MOTOR

- Your child can put a round peg into the correct hole.

- Your child tries to fit one thing inside another.

17 months
GROSS MOTOR

- Your child has more control over stopping and turning when she walks.

- Your child likes to push carriages rather than sit in them.

FINE MOTOR

- Your child may roll a ball to others and pick up objects in motion.

- Your child can toss a ball more accurately.

18 months
GROSS MOTOR

- Your child keeps her feet closer together when walking; her gait becomes much smoother.

- Your child may walk up stairs with you.

- Your child may walk on tiptoe.

FINE MOTOR
- Your child can sort many shapes and drop them into the corresponding holes.

- Your child can take toys apart and put them back together.

- Your child can unzip zippers.

19 months
GROSS MOTOR
- Your child is active and adventuresome throughout the day.

- Your child walks, climbs, trots, and runs whenever possible.

FINE MOTOR
- Your child may be able to stack three or four blocks.

- Your child loves to inspect new objects and places.

- Your child tries to climb out of bed.

- Your child may take off her socks and shoes.

20 months
GROSS MOTOR
- Your child may kick a ball without falling or tripping.

- Your child likes to hang from bars by her hands.

- Your child may climb onto an adult-size chair, pivot around, and sit down.

- Your child may look stiff while running; she may have trouble stopping and maneuvering corners while running.

- Your child tries to jump with both feet, but she may not get off the ground.

FINE MOTOR
- Your child can throw a ball overhand instead of tossing it.

21 months

GROSS MOTOR
- Your child looks down while walking to sidestep obstacles.

- Your child may walk up stairs, holding on to a rail, with both feet on one step.

FINE MOTOR
- Your child may turn the pages of a book one at a time.

- Your child enjoys finger painting and scribbling with big crayons.

- Your child loves to inspect tiny objects, especially bugs.

- Your child shows a preference for her right or left hand.

22 months

GROSS MOTOR

- Your child alternates easily between walking and running, sitting and standing.

- Your child likes to be pushed on a swing and enjoys other playground activities.

FINE MOTOR

- Your child may put on her shoes, though often on the wrong feet.

- Your child tries to buckle her car seat belt.

23 months

GROSS MOTOR

- Your child shows greater coordination in movement.

- Your child often runs rather than walks.

- Your child can seat herself at a table and climb into her car seat on her own.

- Your child may throw a ball into a basket.

FINE MOTOR

- Your child likes to play with clay.

- Your child may draw a crude circle if shown how.

24 months

GROSS MOTOR

- Your child moves with greater efficiency.

- Your child is sturdier on her feet and less likely to fall.

- Your child may be able to walk up and down stairs by herself; some children still feel more comfortable crawling on the steps.

- Your child may enjoy dancing to music; she may learn how to move according to tempo.

25 to 29 months

GROSS MOTOR

- Your child is constantly on the move.

- Your child loves to be chased.

- Your child enjoys going down slides, swinging, and running around playgrounds.

- Your child may be able to pedal a small tricycle.

- Your child may be able to stand on one foot.

- Your child may count stairs and jump off the final step.

- Your child may jump in place, though this takes great effort and coordination.

FINE MOTOR

- Your child learns to coordinate movements of her wrist, fingers, and palm.

- Your child may unscrew lids, turn knobs, and unwrap paper packages.

30 to 36 months

GROSS MOTOR

- Your child's walking becomes more adultlike, with a heel-to-toe gait.

- Your child likes to try out new types of movements, such as like galloping and trotting.

- Your child may alternate feet when climbing up stairs.

- Your child is capable of multiple actions when moving. For example, she can throw a ball while running or eat ice cream while walking.

- Your child can bend over easily without falling.

- Your child can kick a ball with reasonable precision.

- Your child may hit a baseball if it's placed on a stand.

- Your child can pedal and steer a tricycle well.

FINE MOTOR

- Your child can make vertical, horizontal, and circular strokes with crayons.

- Your child can build a tower of six blocks.

- Your child can hold a pencil using the proper writing position.

Red Flags: Warning Signs of Delayed Motor Development

Although each baby develops in her own way and at her own rate, failure to reach certain milestones may signal medical or developmental problems requiring special attention. If you notice any of the following warning signs in your infant, discuss them with your pediatrician.

BIRTH TO 1 MONTH

- Your child sucks poorly and feeds slowly.

- Your child does not blink when shown a bright light.

- Your child does not focus and follow a nearby object moving side to side.

- Your child rarely moves her arms and legs; she seems stiff.

- Your child seems excessively loose in the limbs, or floppy.

- Your child's lower jaw trembles constantly, even when she is not crying or excited.

- Your child does not respond to loud sounds.

1 TO 3 MONTHS

- Your child does not notice her hands by two months.

- Your child does not smile at the sound of your voice by two months.

- Your child does not follow moving objects with her eyes by two to three months.

- Your child does not grasp and hold objects by three months.

- Your child does not smile at people by three months.

- Your child cannot support her head well at three months.

- Your child does not reach for and grasp toys by three to four months.

- Your child has trouble moving one or both eyes in all directions.

- Your child crosses her eyes most of the time (occasional crossing of the eyes is normal in the first few months).

- Your child does not pay attention to new faces, or seems very frightened by new faces or surroundings.

4 TO 7 MONTHS

- Your child still has the Moro reflex after four months.

- Your child seems to have very stiff muscles.

- Your child seems floppy, like a rag doll.

- Your child's head still flops back when her body is pulled up to a sitting position.

- Your child reaches with one hand only.

- Your child refuses to cuddle with you.

- Your child shows no affection for the person who cares for her.

- Your child does not seem to enjoy being around people.

- One or both of your child's eyes consistently turn in or out.

- Your child experiences persistent tearing, eye drainage, or sensitivity to light.

- Your child does not respond to sounds around her.

- Your child has difficulty getting objects to her mouth.

- Your child does not turn her head to locate sounds by four months.

- Your child begins babbling, but does not try to imitate any of your sounds by four months.

- Your child does not push down with her legs when her feet are placed on a firm surface by four months.

- Your child does not roll over in either direction (front to back or back to front) by six months.

- Your child seems inconsolable at night after five months.

- Your child doesn't smile spontaneously by five months.

- Your child cannot sit with help by six months.

- Your child does not laugh or make squealing sounds by six months.

- Your child does not actively reach for objects by six to seven months.

- Your child does not follow objects with both eyes at near (one foot) and far (six feet) ranges by seven months.

- Your child does not bear some weight on her legs by seven months. .

- Your child does not try to attract attention through her actions by seven months.

8 TO 12 MONTHS

- Your child does not crawl.

- Your child drags one side of her body while crawling (for more than one month).

- Your child cannot stand when supported.

- Your child does not search for objects that are hidden while she watches.

- Your child says no single word ("mamma" or "dada").

- Your child does not babble by eight months of age.

- Your child shows no interest in games like peekaboo by eight months.

- Your child has not learned to use gestures, such as waving and shaking her head.

- Your child does not point to objects or pictures when asked.

1 TO 2 YEARS

- Your child cannot walk by eighteen months.

- Your child fails to develop a mature heel-to-toe walking gait after several months of walking, or she walks exclusively on her toes.

- Your child does not speak at least fifteen words by eighteen months.

- Your child does not use two-word sentences by age two.

- Your child does not seem to know the function of common household objects (phone, spoon, toothbrush) by fifteen months.

- Your child does not imitate actions or words by the end of her second year.

- Your child does not follow simple instructions by age two.

- Your child cannot push a wheeled toy by age two.

2 TO 3 YEARS

- Your child falls frequently or has difficulty climbing stairs.

- Your child drools persistently or has very unclear speech.

- Your child is unable to build a tower of more than four blocks.

- Your child has difficulty manipulating small objects.

- Your child is unable to copy a circle by age three.

- Your child is unable to communicate in short phrases.

- Your child has no interest in "pretend" play.

- Your child seems unable to understand simple instructions.

- Your child has little or no interest in other children.

- Your child experiences severe separation anxiety.

7 • Chaos to Order

Music, Math, Science, and Spatial Relations

Before your baby is born, she spends her time in a noisy and rhythmic environment inside your womb, where the amniotic fluid conducts and amplifies the gurgles and pulses and heartbeat occurring inside Mom's gut. While digestive noises may not seem particularly melodic to the average adult, this auditory stimulation actually lays the groundwork for a child's inherent interest in music.

Evidence suggests that newborns respond to music and show a particular appreciation for rhythm. Researchers tested the musical preferences of newborns by analyzing their sucking patterns. They found that babies increased their rate of sucking on a pacifier when the sucking produced rhythmic folk music, but they stopped sucking and made efforts to avoid nonrhythmic noise.

Infants can't dance, but they do bounce to music starting at four to six months. Researchers have found that babies recognize melodies and tunes, as well as changes in pitch or tempo, at this age. Infants prefer to listen to music in natural musical phrases; they find it disconcerting when a composition is stopped in the middle.

A number of studies show that music helps to wire the brain for improved performance in mathematics, science, and spatial relations. Albert Einstein's mother, Pauline, was a devoted musician, and Albert began to study violin before age six. While he did not become a well-known musician, his early music experience almost certainly helped lay the neural foundation for his later accomplishments in mathematics and physics.

The following sections contain suggestions for enhancing your child's abilities in music, math, science, and spatial reasoning through play.

ENHANCING YOUR CHILD'S MUSICAL ABILITY

Offer your infant the soothing sound of your heartbeat. After hearing their mother's steady heartbeat for months in utero, many children find this rhythmic pulse a comfort after birth. In fact, an obstetrician at the University of Tokyo inserted a tiny microphone into the dilated cervix of a woman beginning labor. His recording of the sounds of the womb indicated that the mother's pounding heart and the rush of blood through her arteries was the loudest sound the baby heard. After birth, he played the recorded sounds back to the newborn, who soon calmed and fell asleep after hearing the familiar sounds.

If your newborn suffers from colic or tends to be difficult to soothe, try making a recording of your own heartbeat. (Commercially prepared recordings are available, but your baby may find your heartbeat more reassuring, since this is the rhythm she became accustomed to in the womb.) Bring a tape recorder to a prenatal or postpartum obstetric visit and ask your doctor to use the Doppler, or Doptone, to amplify the sound of your heartbeat so that it can easily be recorded.

Play a little background music.

Researchers have found that music can improve our moods, make us work more efficiently, and make learning easier. The Bulgarian psychiatrist Georgi Lozanov argues that music facilitates learning by putting people in the "concert state," meaning that they are physically relaxed and mentally alert. In this state, the brain can acquire new information in a relaxed and enjoyable fashion.

Studies have found that music helps babies gain weight, develop motor coordination, and cry less. In addition, it has been shown to stimulate creativity. Classical music is so effective at soothing babies and regulating unstable fetal heartbeats that it is played in the nurseries at a number of major hospitals. In Florida all state-financed child-care centers and preschools must play classical music to their students. Babies born in Georgia actually leave the hospital with an audiocassette or compact disc package from the governor, which states, "Build Your Baby's Brain Through the Power of Music!"

The most effective compositions tend to be soothing, classical pieces; hard rock, which tends to agitate babies (and many adults), is least effective. Many experts recommend the Baby B's: Bach, Beethoven, and Brahms. The following list includes a number of compositions your child may enjoy.

Music to Learn By

BACH	Symphony in C Major
	Symphony in D Major
	Air on G String
	"Jesu Joy of Man's Desiring"
	Prelude and Fugue in G Minor
	Fantasy in C Minor
	Trio in D Minor
BEETHOVEN	Concerto in E-flat Major for Piano and Orchestra, op. 73, no. 5
	Concerto for Violin and Orchestra in D Major
	"Für Elise"
BRAHMS	Concerto for Violin and Orchestra in D Major, op. 77
CHOPIN	Waltzes
CORELLI	Concerti Grossi, opp. 4, 10, 11, 12
	Concerti Grossi, op. 6, nos. 3, 5, 8, 9

HANDEL	Concerto for Organ and Orchestra
	Water Music
	Concerti Grossi, op. 3, nos. 1, 2, 3, 5
HAYDN	Symphony no. 67 in F Major
	Concerto for Violin and String Orchestra no. 1 in C Major
	Concerto for Violin and String Orchestra no. 2 in G Major
MOZART	Haffner Symphony
	Prague Symphony
	Concertó for Piano and Orchestra no. 18 in B-flat Major
	Concerto for Violin and Orchestra
	Concerto no. 7 in D Major for Piano
PACHELBEL	Canon in D Major
TCHAIKOVSKY	Concerto no. 1 in B-flat Minor for Piano and Orchestra
VIVALDI	*The Four Seasons*
	Five Concerti for Flute and Chamber Orchestra

Sing to your child (even if you don't have a fabulous voice).

Many parents choose to add a song or two to the nightly bedtime story. By regularly singing with your child, you are teaching her the importance and enjoyment of music. Even just rhythmically tapping your child's knee or clapping your hands can teach your child to recognize and appreciate the beat. As your baby becomes a toddler, tap out the rhythm of nursery rhymes, lullabies, and kiddie songs to reinforce the rhythm of language.

Allow your child to experience music.

All children have significant musical abilities at birth, but most children are not given the opportunity to cultivate their gifts. Small children use rhythm in almost everything they do—their movement, their speech, their ability to repeat melodies and rhythmic patterns.

A child's musical ability becomes apparent during the preschool years. Almost all four-year-olds have perfect pitch, but most lose this ability by age seven. (Never fear: the ability to identify pitch can be relearned or reinforced with training.) In addition, children also have a well-toned inner ear; they can hear tones in their head as if they were listening to them being played out loud.

If your child has an interest in music, formal training can be an excellent way of developing her skills while at the same time shaping her neural pathways for improved spatial intelligence. Studies have shown that early music training can improve a child's ability to reason, to work mazes and puzzles, to draw geometric figures, and to visualize the world. These abstract skills can be applied later as higher mathematics, problem solving, and engineering.

Studies have found that music training actually changes the structure of the brain. German researchers used magnetic resonance imaging (MRI) technology to examine the brains of nine people who played string instruments. The amount of the brain dedicated to the use of the thumb and pinkie of the left hand (the fingers used when playing a stringed instrument) was significantly greater in the musicians than in people who did not play. Interestingly, the most important factor in determining the amount of brain space designated to their skill was not the total amount of time spent rehearsing with the instrument but rather the age at which the person began playing. The earlier a person began playing an instrument, the greater the brain space dedicated to playing it.

Other studies have shown that music training helps improve a child's spatial reasoning ability. For example, researchers at the University of California, Irvine, studied nineteen three- to five-year-olds who received weekly training on the keyboard and sang daily in a chorus. They compared these children with fifteen others of the same age who did not receive any music training. After eight months, the children taking music lessons were found to have "dramatically improved spatial reasoning," and they scored as much as 80 percent higher in spatial intelligence than the children who did not receive music lessons.

Experience music as a family.

Make special family outings to concerts, music recitals, operas, and other musical events. Let different family members choose the events so that everyone can learn to appreciate a different musical tradition. In addition to attending musical performances, take time to sing together, to listen to music together, and to dance to favorite musical compositions.

What Kind of Music Lessons Are Best for Your Child?

Teaching a small child to appreciate music and to play an instrument takes patience and skill. While many local music teachers may offer an effective program of instruction, there are several well-known national children's music programs, including the Suzuki, Yamaha, Orff-Schulwerk, and Kodály methods. Each has a different approach to teaching.

Suzuki Talent Education Program: This method teaches the child to play a specific musical instrument, typically the violin or piano. The technique was developed by the Japanese violinist Shinichi Suzuki before World War II. Children can begin playing at age two or three, and so, not surprisingly, the program relies heavily on parental involvement and reinforcement. Children are taught to play by ear (rather than use musical notation) and to echo or play back a musical recording by regular practice. For more information, contact the Suzuki Association of the Americas, P.O. Box 17310, Boulder, CO 80308; (303) 444-0948.

Yamaha Method: This technique was developed in the 1950s by the Japanese makers of Yamaha pianos. Children from the ages of four to six receive instruction in groups of six to twelve students. Parents attend classes with their children and reinforce the lessons at home. For children under age six, the program emphasizes singing, ear training, and learning to identify simple melodies and rhythms. After age six, children begin to learn to play the piano and simple rhythm instruments. For more information, contact Yamaha Music, 6600 Orangethorpe Avenue, Buena Park, CA 90620; (714) 522-9011.

Music for Young Children: This approach is very much like the Yamaha method. For more information, contact Music for Young Children, 39 Leacock Way, Kanata, Ontario, Canada K2K 1T1; (800) 561-1692.

Orff-Schulwerk Approach: German composer Carl Orff developed this approach to music instruction in the 1920s. The program teaches informal music making rather than the performance of specific compositions. Children learn simple music notation, but they do so by snapping their fingers, stomping their feet, slapping their thighs, and playfully echoing songs as part of music games. For more information, contact the American Orff-Schulwerk Associations, P.O. Box 391089, Cleveland, OH 44139-8089; (440) 543-5366.

Kodály Education: Hungarian composer Zoltán Kodály developed this approach to music instruction to bring music to the masses rather than just the elite. The program uses a cappella singing to teach musical rhymes, folk melodies, and games. The program is used in most Hungarian schools. For more information, contact the Organization of American Kodály Educators, Music Department, Box 2017, Nicholls State University, Thibodaux, LA 70310; (504) 448-4602.

No matter which type of instruction you choose, you should make sure your child wants to take formal music instruction before signing her up. Consider sitting in on one or two lessons (perhaps with two or more different programs) so that your child can choose the program she would most enjoy.

Start with a short-term commitment, perhaps four or five one-hour classes. After that point, discuss the program with your child and ask if she would like to continue. If your child is still interested, have her commit to taking lessons for the remainder of the semester or season.

ENHANCING YOUR CHILD'S MATH ABILITY THROUGH PLAY

Play is the highest level of child development. It is the spontaneous expression of thought and feeling. It is the purest creation of the child's mind as it is also a pattern and copy of the natural life hidden in man and in all things.

—FRIEDRICH FROEBEL,
nineteenth-century German educator and
the originator of the kindergarten

Play games with your child.

Simple board games like Candyland and Chutes and Ladders allow your child to read the numbers on the dice and to count the spaces as she moves her playing piece over the board. Dominoes teaches children about numbers and patterns. Checkers and tic-tac-toe teach your child about game strategy and anticipating her opponent's moves. Clue requires your child to record evidence and use logic to determine who committed a crime. Take time during play to help your child understand the mathematical concept being applied in the game. If your child is too young to play alone, pair up with her and help her learn to take turns and engage in fair play.

Teach your child to sort items into categories.
At snack time, ask your child to sort the M&M's into different colors. When folding laundry, ask your child to divide the socks by color or size. If your child has moved beyond the everything-goes-into-the-mouth stage, give her a pile of buttons and coins and ask her to divide them into her own categories, using an old egg carton as a convenient container for sorting.

Search for shapes.
Tell your child about different shapes and their characteristics, then look through the house for objects of different shapes. Where can she find a triangle? How about a circle? At lunch, cut your child's sandwich into squares one day and triangles the next. Once your child has mastered the circle, square, and triangle, move on to pentagons, octagons, and parallelograms. (Your child will probably understand these shapes better if you draw them or cut them out of paper.)

Allow your child to experiment with time.
Your child will have little conception of time until you teach her. Measurements of time are essentially meaningless to children until they understand the passage of time in a way that is relevant to their experience. For example, one minute becomes the length of time it takes to walk around the house one time and ten seconds becomes the time it takes to

walk up the stairs and back down. A half hour is the length of your child's favorite television program. You and your child can have fun and begin to appreciate the measurement of time by using a stopwatch or a watch with a second hand to time various activities. Using this technique, even small children will learn that ten seconds is a short amount of time and ten minutes is considerably longer.

Measure everything in sight.
Give your child a ruler or a tape measure and experiment with measuring the things in your child's world. How long is her bed? How long is her foot? This simple exercise will help your child develop a basic appreciation for distances, in addition to helping her learn that there are twelve inches in one foot.

You can also give your child a set of measuring cups and spoons and let her play in the sink. You can ask an older child how many cups of water will fit in a gallon bottle, or how many half cups fit into a whole cup.

Weigh everything your child can lift.
Allow your child to learn about relative weights by weighing different objects. Which weighs more, a book or a shoe? A cup of rice or a baked potato? Your child will begin to experience—and therefore appreciate—the meaning of heavy and light, one pound and one ounce.

Get over your math anxiety.
If you tell your child that you "don't like math" you're setting her up for failure. Remember, you are your child's most important role model. In addition, be careful not to send your daughter the message "boys are better in math than girls" or

"most girls don't do well in math," because these negative expectations can become self-fulfilling prophecies. Instead, expect your child to do well. Even if you are barely able to add and subtract without the aid of a calculator, keep in mind that your child's abilities and interests will be different from yours.

Cook with your child.

Cooking is an excellent way to teach your child about measuring, sequencing, fractions, and other mathematical concepts. Little children love to help out in the kitchen, and there is a great deal they can learn there. *Bon appétit.*

Take your child with you to the grocery store.

Talk about prices and sizes of food. Look at different shaped packages in the store. The more you engage your child in the activity of shopping, the better behaved she is apt to be as you wander the aisles.

ENHANCING YOUR CHILD'S SCIENCE ABILITY THROUGH PLAY

Allow children to engage in hands-on learning.

Children naturally employ basic scientific method as they explore their environment. They intuitively ask questions, form hypotheses, experiment to test those hypotheses, and come up with ideas about how the world works.

Science is interesting and fun when children are allowed to experience it firsthand. This natural preference for active learning was demonstrated in Mesa, Arizona, when seventh graders were allowed to either continue science or opt for electives when they entered junior high school. Fully 96 percent of the kids who had been involved in hands-on science programs chose to continue taking science, while only 4 percent of the kids in traditional textbook-oriented programs chose to continue taking science.

Let the facts teach themselves.

Every time you set out to explore the natural world, don't feel that you must lecture your child about specific facts and scientific principles. Instead, let your child ask questions and practice the skills of careful observation. By practicing these important skills, your child will discover the answers herself—and the experience will be much more meaningful. (Of course, you can fill your child in on some scientific principles, but do so only when your child is ready and only to clarify what she is observing and having trouble putting into words.) The learning process should be driven by the child's interest in learning, not the parent's interest in teaching.

Ask your child open-ended questions.

Why do you think it is important to recycle? What do you think will happen to that snowman when the sun comes out? By asking questions that do not have yes or no answers, you child must consider the evidence and formulate a more thoughtful response. Teaching your child to question and to try to make sense of what she observes is the essence of scientific inquiry.

Engage in Scientific Exploration with Your Child.

Go to the library and check out a book on science experiments for kids. Here are a few popular activities that don't require special equipment:

Will it sink or float? Fill the sink or bathtub with water. Go through the house with your child and collect objects that won't be damaged by a little bit of water (stones, Styrofoam plates, pencils, soap, a wooden spoon, a metal spoon). Ask your child whether she thinks the object will sink or float—then let her discover the answer.

How do seeds grow? Collect seeds from grapefruits, apples, seed packets, and your yard. Wrap them in several layers of paper towel or cheesecloth, place them in a sunny window, and keep them moist. Wait four or five days and then look to see which seeds have sprouted. If you feel ambitious, plant the sprouted seed and try to grow a plant.

How do you make orange? Teach your child about colors and color mixing by using either watercolor paints or food coloring as a base. Use a Styrofoam egg carton and fill the compartments with a half inch of water. Mix the colors into the clear water and observe the color changes. How do you make orange? (By mixing yellow and red.) How about purple?

What will the magnet do? Buy two inexpensive magnets at a toy store and allow your child to go through the house touching the magnet to various household surfaces. (WARNING: Don't let her put the magnet near your computer or she may damage the machine.) Does the magnet stick to the refrigerator? The cabinet? The dining room table? Then give your child the other magnet and allow her to experiment with the two of them. Do they attract one another or push each other away?

Take a closer look. Dig through the junk drawer to find a simple magnifying lens or pick one up at a toy store. Let your child explore the world with her new eyes. What does skin look like up close? How about a leaf? An ant? A bagel?

How much did it rain last night? Your child will be fascinated to learn how much water is produced during a rainstorm. Make a rain gauge or simply put an old plastic container out in the yard before a rainstorm. When the weather breaks, retrieve the container and look at how much rainwater is inside. Is there more than your child expected? Less?

Where is the moon tonight? If the weather forecast is for clear skies, take your child outside in the early evening to watch the moon. Repeat the process nightly for a week or more and notice how the moon changes shape. What does a full moon look like? How does it look as it gets smaller?

ENHANCING YOUR CHILD'S SPATIAL REASONING THROUGH PLAY

Play with blocks.

Allow your child to play with blocks of different sizes and colors. By manipulating the blocks, your child will fine-tune her sense of spatial relations. Your child will learn that to stack one block on top of another, she must center the blocks one atop the other. She will also discover that she cannot balance a large block on top of a small block. These basic truths about spatial relations can best be understood through firsthand experience.

Play with stacking "donuts" and other toys with graduated sizes.

These toys teach your child about relative sizes, including the concept that one object fits between its larger neighbor on one side and its smaller neighbor on the other. This seemingly unimportant concept is actually a cornerstone of counting, because it lays the foundation for serialization, the concept of one item following another.

Let your child play with water, sand, and clay.

These sensual experiences allow your child to experience firsthand the concepts of space and volume. As your child pours water from a large container into a smaller one, she will learn that the result is a small flood. This messy play is not only fun but also essential for later development of spatial reasoning and mathematic abilities.

Let your child steer.

In order to develop their conceptual mapping skills, children need to climb, crawl, and explore different paths. By physically exploring their world, children learn to understand relationships involving distance and space.

Children who explore on their own tend to develop better spatial abilities than those who simply follow a parent or older sibling. In a study of thirty-two two- to three-and-a-half-year-olds, the children either freely explored a specially designed playhouse or were guided by their parents. When it came time to reverse their path and leave the play-house, the children who had initiated the exploration found it much easier to get out than those who passively followed a guide. So allow your child to experience self-directed play as much as possible.

Let your girl act like a boy.
Boys tend to do better than girls in tests of spatial relations, and some experts theorize that the types of toys and games boys play may enhance these skills. One study of girls who excelled in math and science found that as children they were allowed to play with "boys' toys," to explore on their own, and to solve their own problems. Those children—both boys and girls—who depended on their parents to lead them and who tended to play passively earned lower scores in math and spatial relations. To enhance your child's abili-ties, encourage her independence and allow her to explore with few restraints.

8 · Food for Thought

Making Intelligent Food Choices

It's impossible to overestimate the importance of a well-balanced diet when it comes to maximizing your child's intellectual potential. In fact, the nourishment your child receives in the womb and during the first three years of life has a critical impact on brain growth, regardless of the stimulation and enrichment she receives at home.

The food choices a woman makes during pregnancy lay the groundwork for fetal brain development. Poor nutrition leaves the developing baby without the nutrients necessary to grow a healthy brain. Studies have shown that mothers who eat an inadequate diet during pregnancy tend to have babies with brains that are smaller, not as well myelinated, and not as well developed in terms of dendrite connections, compared with the brains of babies who were well fed in the womb. The babies also tend to suffer from serious and often fatal problems, such as spina bifida (unenclosed spinal cord), anencephaly (missing brain), and microcephaly (very small brain).

After birth, these malnourished infants tend to suffer from mental retardation, poor motor coordination, difficulty forming relationships, and impaired physical growth; they also stand a more significant risk of dying during their first year. It appears that malnutrition is most harmful during the last trimester of pregnancy, when the baby is growing rapidly and the brain is growing and forming essential neurological connections.

Some of the most dramatic research on prenatal nutrition was conducted during World War II on women who were suffering from malnutrition. The babies of these women were found to have a 169 percent increase in brain and central nervous system defects, compared with the infants of women who received adequate nutrition.

More recently, researchers have actually measured the impact of diet on IQ. A study conducted by researchers at the Boston University School of Medicine and published in the *Journal of the American Academy of Child Psychiatry* in January 1983 found that a poor diet lowers a child's IQ by an average of 12 points, regardless of the type of stimulation the child receives at home. The researchers measured the intelligence of malnourished children in Barbados and compared their scores with those of children from similar backgrounds and social conditions who received an adequate diet.

After a child is born, her diet continues to shape her mental development. Poor nutrition can impair a child's intellectual development, but if the child receives adequate nutrition (as well as intellectual and social stimulation) before the age of three, in many cases she can make significant strides toward reaching normal development.

The following suggestions can help you provide your

child with the nutrients necessary to reach her intellectual potential. Of course, work with your obstetrician during pregnancy and your child's pediatrician after delivery to customize a diet plan to meet the individual needs of you and your child.

FEEDING YOUR CHILD BEFORE BIRTH

Eat extra protein.

The brain is made up largely of protein. In order to have the raw material required for optimal fetal brain development, a pregnant woman should consume about twice the normal amount of dietary protein as she would before conception. The average American eats about 43 grams of protein a day. The goal for a pregnant woman should be about 80 grams daily.

Good Food Sources of Protein

Skim or low-fat milk or buttermilk, low-fat cottage cheese, yogurt, cheese, eggs, meat and poultry, fish and seafood, and tofu. You can also create complete protein combinations by combining legumes (such as peanut butter, beans, black-eyed peas, soybeans, chickpeas, lentils, and split peas) with grains (such as rice, barley, millet, pasta, oats, nuts, and wheat germ).

Take a nutrition supplement.

Most obstetricians recommend that their patients take prenatal nutrition supplements to ensure that they receive all of the vitamins and minerals necessary during pregnancy. Vitamin and mineral deficiencies can result in a number of birth defects.

As a general rule, nutrition supplements are best absorbed when taken with other foods. You can also enhance the nutrition content of the foods you eat by choosing fresh or frozen vegetables (the nutrients in canned vegetables tend to leach out into the packing water), by eating fruits and vegetables with their skins on (when appropriate, and after washing, of course), and by pressure-cooking, steaming, or stir-frying vegetables to minimize the cooking time.

Take supplemental B vitamins.
The B vitamins are essential for brain functioning. They are water-soluble, meaning that they are not stored in the body very long, so you need to consume them on a regular basis.

An inadequate amount of folic acid (a B vitamin) can cause neural tube defects in a developing baby. Vitamin B_{12} is essential for the formation of the myelin sheath around the nerve fibers in the brain and spinal cord. The other B vitamins also help to convert proteins, carbohydrates, and fats into fuel, among other functions. There are seven B vitamins, and they are all important for proper fetal growth.

Most obstetricians recommend that their pregnant patients take at least 400 micrograms of folic acid as part of an overall supplement. Discuss with your doctor the issue of taking an additional B-complex supplement, in addition to a multivitamin, multimineral supplement.

Good Food Sources of B Vitamins
Barley, beans, bee pollen, beef, brewer's yeast, cheese, eggs, fish and seafood, liver, nuts, oats, rice bran, seeds, sesame seeds, wheat germ.

Drink at least eight 8-ounce glasses of water daily.
When pregnant you can't afford to skimp on fluids. During pregnancy your body's demands for fluids increase. The fluids can minimize your chances of developing constipation, and they help wash toxins and waste products from your body. While it might seem counterintuitive, the extra fluids can help to reduce swelling. Drink at least eight cups of water, or more if you're retaining water.

Keep in mind that you don't have to consume water alone. Milk, fruit and vegetable juices, decaffeinated coffee and tea, and soup all count toward your total. Try to spread the fluid intake out over the day.

Follow a well-balanced diet plan.
During pregnancy you need to add about three hundred calories to your regular diet to provide the additional nutrients your baby needs. The following pregnancy eating plan offers a general guide to eating for two:

Protein: Four 2- to 3-ounce servings of proteins, such as meat, poultry, fish, eggs, beans, nuts, peanut butter, dried peas, or tofu

Milk and Dairy Products: Four 8-ounce servings of milk or dairy products, such as skim or low-fat milk, low-fat cottage cheese or yogurt. A serving of cheese would be 1½ ounces of natural cheese or 2 ounces of processed cheese.

Breads, Cereals, and Grains: Six to eleven servings of breads, cereals, and grains, such as whole-grain breads, oatmeal, cracked-wheat cereals, rice, potatoes, muffins, or tortillas

Cruciferous and Dark Green Leafy Vegetables: Three to five servings of broccoli, Brussels sprouts, dark green leafy vegetables, such as spinach, romaine lettuce, cauliflower, or collard greens. One serving would equal 1 cup of raw leafy vegetables or ½ cup of cooked or raw, yellow vegetables.

Vitamin C–Rich Fruits and Vegetables: Two to four half-cup servings of vitamin C–rich foods, such as strawberries, citrus fruits or juices, peppers, tomatoes, cabbage, cantaloupes, or papayas

Other Fruits and Vegetables: Two to three half-cup servings of apples, grapes, corn, or other fruits and vegetables

FEEDING YOUR BABY AFTER BIRTH

Breast-feed if you can.
Breast-feeding helps to meet your child's physical and emotional needs. Breast milk not only provides the nutrients necessary for brain development but also lowers a child's risk of developing allergies, ear infections, respiratory infections, diarrhea, eczema, pneumonia, bacterial meningitis, and other medical problems. The physical closeness and intimate contact during nursing also strengthens the emotional bond between mother and child.

A number of studies have demonstrated that breast-feeding boosts brain development; it is exquisite brain food. Some show a "small but detectable" rise in cognitive development, while others show as much as an 8-point increase in IQ when comparing breast-and bottle-fed babies. One study published in 1992 found that premature babies who were tube-fed breast milk expressed by their mothers developed much faster than babies tube-fed commercial formula. Another study that compared 1,291 breast-fed babies with 1,133 bottle-fed babies found that the breast-fed children scored significantly higher on intelligence and reading tests at eight years of age.

While formula manufacturers strive to replicate Mother Nature's secret recipe, researchers do not fully understand the exact nutritional profile of the foods that are responsible for brain development. The complex mixture of long-chain fatty acids, proteins, amino acids, and enzymes that make up breast milk cannot be duplicated in a laboratory. Still, formula manufacturers continue to tinker with the nutrients they add to their products in an attempt to create the best commercial product possible. One ingredient that may make a difference in brain development is taurine, a substance that promotes brain and nerve development. It is not found in all types of commercial formula, so if you choose to bottle-feed look for a brand that contains taurine.

Despite the known benefits of breast-feeding, in 1995 just 59 percent of American women breast-fed (either exclusively or in conjunction with bottle-feeding) at the time they left the hospital, and a mere 21 percent were nursing when their babies were six months old. Unfortunately, the United States has one of the lowest rates of breast-feeding in the world.

The American Academy of Pediatrics recommends breast-feeding for at least one year. Many pediatricians extend that recommendation to two years, since children as old as two can benefit from the fatty acids and antibodies found in breast milk. Of course, long-term breast-feeding isn't for everyone. If possible, try to nurse your child for a minimum of four to six months so that your newborn can get the best nutritional start possible. When the child is four to six months old your pediatrician may suggest you introduce solid foods. The solid food diet should reflect the same nutrient ratios as breast milk: 50 percent fats, 35 to 45 percent complex carbohydrates, and 5 to 15 percent proteins.

Nursing also offers other secondary benefits to both mother and child. The baby will experience a range of taste sensations that will broaden her sensory world. Newborns have a well-developed sense of taste and smell; the flavor of breast milk changes daily with the mother's diet. The wide variety of flavors provided by breast milk introduces the child to a range of new flavors long before she is ready for solid foods. Breast-feeding also reduces a woman's risk of developing ovarian and premenopausal breast cancer, osteoporosis, and other medical conditions.

Give your child a daily nutrition supplement.
Talk to your child's pediatrician about what type of multivitamin, multimineral supplement is best for your child. Do not assume that a daily pill can take the place of balanced meals, but nutrition supplements can provide some assurance that your child is receiving the minimal nutrients necessary for proper growth and development.

Feed your child breakfast every day.

Your mother was right: your child—and you—should start every morning with a good, hearty breakfast. Children who skip breakfast tend to consume fewer vitamins and minerals over the course of the day, according to a recent summary of a twenty-five-year-long heart study.

Breakfast is quite literally brain food; it provides the body with the blood sugar or glucose necessary to fuel the brain at the start of the day. The brain uses up about two-thirds of the body's glucose or sugar; it burns this fuel both day and night. Within as little as thirty minutes of a drop in blood glucose levels, the brain can grow sluggish. To keep your child's brain working at its peak, it needs a sufficient supply of glucose.

A number of studies have demonstrated that children (and adults) perform better at intellectual tasks if they have breakfast. One study conducted at the University of Texas Health Science Center in Houston found that children who ate breakfast made measurably fewer errors in their schoolwork as the morning wore on, compared with children who skipped their morning meal. While the research hasn't focused on the diet of the three-and-under set, it seems reasonable to assume that younger children also learn better when they eat a balanced breakfast.

If your child doesn't have much interest in food in the morning, offer a glass of milk or a bowl of cereal. Over time, add fruit, juice, or yogurt. If the problem involves too little time to pause and enjoy a nourishing breakfast, it makes sense to reset the alarm clock and wake up fifteen or twenty minutes earlier. You may miss the few minutes of shut-eye, but your child's body and brain will benefit in the long run.

Avoid food additives.

Young children can react negatively to food additives, including artificial sweeteners (such as aspartame and saccharine), flavor enhancers (such as monosodium glutamate), preservatives (such as nitrites), artificial colors, and artificial flavors. The negative reactions can include poor concentration, fidgeting, short attention span, excitability, impulsive behavior, aggression, clumsiness, and insomnia. To avoid these problems, read food labels carefully and avoid products containing these additives.

Don't restrict your child's fat intake.

Young children need a significant amount of dietary fat for healthy brain development. Fat is the dietary source of acetylcholine, a neurotransmitter that helps maintain the cell membranes in the nerves. Without enough dietary fat, the nerve cell membranes become brittle and damaged, decreasing overall brain function.

For optimal brain development, do not restrict your child's fat intake for the first two years. When your child consumes cow's milk, choose whole milk rather than low-fat or skim. At age two, talk to your child's pediatrician about switching to skim milk and limiting other sources of animal fat (which can elevate cholesterol levels).

Be sure your child receives a sufficient amount of dietary iron.

A child who does not receive enough dietary iron (or has trouble absorbing the iron from foods in the diet) may suffer from iron-deficiency anemia, which starves the brain of oxygen. Oxygen is carried to the brain and throughout the body by hemoglobin, the protein that makes blood appear red. An insufficient amount of dietary iron can impair the production and function of hemoglobin. The result: lethargy, a short attention span, difficulty with learning, and impaired concentration.

Fortunately, most cases of iron-deficiency anemia can be reversed with supplemental iron and a change in diet. Many pediatricians recommend that parents give young children daily supplements containing iron. If you are not giving your child supplements and you suspect that your child may be suffering from iron-deficiency anemia, discuss the issue with your child's doctor or health care professional.

MILESTONES IN YOUR CHILD'S EATING HABITS

Birth to 2 months
- Your child may drink three to four ounces of milk at each feeding.

3 to 8 months
- Your child may smack her lips to indicate hunger or to show anticipation of feeding.

- Between four and six months, most children begin to eat pureed solids and cereals.

- Your child may want to begin feeding herself with zwiebacks or other crackers designed for infants.

- By six months, most children eat three meals a day, in addition to two or three snacks a day.

- When your child becomes mobile, she may not gain weight for several weeks or months.

- At eight months, your child may begin drinking from a cup (with spills).

9 to 16 months

- By age one, your child should be ready to hand-feed herself an entire meal. In many cases, children insist on feeding themselves. If she picks up a spoon, she often drops the food before it reaches her mouth.

- Your child begins to exhibit specific food likes and dislikes.

- By twelve to fourteen months, your child may drink less milk, though milk should be included at all meals.

17 to 24 months

- Your child may dawdle during meals.

- By eighteen months, your child may be able to spoon-feed herself more reliably.

- Your child can blow on food when it's hot.

- Your child should drink sixteen to thirty-two ounces of milk a day.

- Your child learns to express her food needs with words like "more" and "all gone."

- By age two, your child may be able to eat most table foods. Your child should be encouraged to use eating utensils.

2 to 3 years

- Your child should eat the same food that the rest of the family eats.

- Sweets should not be used to bribe a child to finish dinner. (In such cases, candy and sweets become even more desirable as a reward.)

- Your child's appetite may fluctuate; she may even skip a meal occasionally.

- Your child should be encouraged to sit through an entire meal with the family.

- By age three, your child should be able to use a fork efficiently, though she will not be able to cut her food into small enough pieces without assistance.

Organizations of Interest

Childhelp USA National Child Abuse Hotline
(800) 4-A-CHILD
This twenty-four-hour crisis hotline for child abuse prevention also offers a parenting resources line. Staffers have graduate degrees in counseling with expertise in parenting issues.

Children's Art Foundation
P.O. Box 83
Santa Cruz, CA 95063
(408) 426-5557, (800) 447-4569
www.stonesoup.com
This group is dedicated to promoting children's artistic and literary expression. It maintains the Museum of Children's Art and publishes *Stone Soup*, a bimonthly periodical of children's artwork and writing (cost: $32 a year).

Children's Television Workshop
One Lincoln Plaza
New York, NY 10023
(212) 595-3456
www.ctw.org
This organization supports research on the use of television for educational purposes. The workshop has developed a

number of children's programs, including *Sesame Street* and *The Electric Company*.

Dana Alliance for Brain Initiatives
1001 G Street, NW, Suite 1025
Washington, DC 20001
(202) 737-9200
www.dana.org
This organization publishes the newsletter *The Brain in the News*, which includes articles and reprints about the brain and neurological research.

Gesell Institute of Child Development
310 Prospect Street
New Haven, CT 06511
(203) 777-3481
One of the oldest and most respected child-development research institutes in the country, the institute offers a number of books, including *Child Behavior, Your One Year Old, Your Two Year Old*, etc.

Institutes for the Achievement of Human Potential
8801 Stenton Avenue
Wyndmoor, PA 19038
(215) 233-2050, (800) 344-MOTHER
www.iahp.org
This organization sponsors programs designed to increase the intelligence of well and brain-injured infants and publishes a number of books on the subject, including *How to Multiply Your Baby's Intelligence* and *What to Do About Your Brain-Injured Child*.

National Association for the Education of Young Children
1509 16th Street, NW
Washington, DC 20036-1426
(202) 232-8777, (800) 424-2460
www.naeyc.org
This association is the nation's largest organization of early childhood professionals dedicated to improving the quality

of education for children from birth to age eight. The group publishes brochures, books, and videos on a variety of educational topics and publishes a monthly journal, *Young Children*.

National Coalition for Music Education
1806 Robert Fulton Drive
Reston, VA 22091
(703) 860-4000
This organization provides parents with information on the benefits of music education for children.

National Parent Information Network
Children's Research Center
51 Gerty Drive
University of Illinois at Urbana
Champaign, IL 61820-7469
(217) 333-1386, (800) 583-4135
(weekdays: 8 A.M.–5 P.M. CST)
www.npin.org
The network is staffed with parenting specialists available to answer questions. In addition, the Education Resource Information Center Clearinghouse on Elementary and Early Childhood Education offers database searches on topics of concern to parents, with an emphasis on issues involving early childhood and elementary education. There is no charge for a database search.

National Parenting Association
65 Central Park West, Suite 1D
New York, NY 10023
(212) 362-7575, (800) 709-8795
The organization provides books and information on parenting skills and issues of concern to parents.

Parents Anonymous
(909) 621-6184
(weekdays: 8 A.M.–4:30 P.M. PST)
The national office refers parents to forty-five state and regional affiliates that offer support groups, counseling, and referrals.

Parents as Teachers National Center
10176 Corporate Square Drive, Suite 230
St. Louis, MO 63132
(314) 432-4330
This voluntary early learning program for parents with children from newborn to age five, is based on the belief that parents are children's first and most important teachers. The group offers training and personalized home visits by certified parent educators, among other services.

Single Parents Association
4727 East Bell Road, Suite 45-209
Phoenix, AZ 85032
(800) 704-2102
(weekdays: 9 A.M.–6 P.M. CST)
www.singleparents.org
This association answers parents' questions about child rearing and helps parents find support groups and resources in their communities.

Zero to Three
734 15th Street, NW
10th Floor
Washington, DC 20005
(202) 638-1144
www.zerotothree.org
This national organization is dedicated to the social, emotional, cognitive, and physical development of children from birth through age three. The organization serves professionals, such as pediatricians, child-care workers, and educators, as well as parents and policymakers.

Web Sites of Interest

ParenTalkNewsletter
www.tnpc.com/parentalk/index.html
This site posts articles prepared by physicians and psychologists. It covers a vast range of topics and information.

ParenthoodWeb
www.parenthoodweb.com
Pediatricians and psychiatrists respond to reader questions posted on e-mail. In addition, the site includes answers posted to a range of questions.

Parenting Q&A
www.parenting-qa.com
This site offers prompt responses to parents' questions and concerns. It offers reading lists for kids, games for rainy days, and other suggestions.

ParentSoup
www.parentsoup.com
This site provides discussion forums on topics of interest to parents, from attention deficit disorder to step-parenting to babies with special needs.

Selected Bibliography

Acredolo, Linda P., and Susan W. Goodwyn. *Baby Signs: How to Talk with Your Baby Before Your Baby Can Talk: Building a Bridge with Baby Signs*. Chicago: Contemporary Books, 1996.

Amabile, Teresa M. *Growing Up Creative*. New York: Crown, 1989.

Armstrong, Thomas, Ph.D. *Awakening Your Child's Natural Genius: Enhancing Curiosity, Creativity, and Learning Ability for Parents of Children Aged 3 to 12*. New York: G. P. Putnam's Sons, 1991.

———. *In Their Own Way: Discovering and Encouraging Your Child's Personal Learning Style*. Los Angeles: Jeremy P. Tarcher, 1987.

———. *Seven Kinds of Smart: Identifying and Developing Your Many Intelligences*. New York: Plume, 1993.

Auerbach, Stevanne. *The Toy Chest: A Sourcebook of Toys for Children*. Secaucus, N.J.: Lyle Stuart, 1986.

Baron, Naomi S. *Growing Up with Language: How Children Learn to Talk*. Reading, Mass.: Addison-Wesley Publishing Co., 1993.

Beck, Joan. *How to Raise a Brighter Child: The Case for Early Learning*. New York: Pocket Books, 1986.

Bloom, Benjamin. *Developing Talent in Young People*. New York: Ballantine, 1985.

Bowlby, John. *A Secure Base: Parent-Child Attachment and Healthy Human Development*. New York: Basic Books, 1990.

Brazelton, T. Berry, M.D. *Infants and Mothers*. New York: Dell, 1979.

————. *Touchpoints: Your Child's Emotional and Behavioral Development*. Reading, Mass.: Addison-Wesley Publishing Co., 1994.

Brookes, Mona. *Drawing with Children*. Los Angeles: Jeremy P. Tarcher, 1986.

Calvin, William H. *How Brains Think: Evolving Intelligence, Then and Now*. New York: Basic Books, 1996.

Caplan, Frank, and Theresa Caplan. *The Power of Play*. Garden City, N.Y.: Anchor Press/Doubleday, 1973.

Children's Television Workshop. *Parents' Guide to Raising Kids Who Love to Learn*. New York: Prentice Hall, 1989.

Clarke, Linda, and Catherine Ireland. *Learning to Talk, Talking to Learn*. New York: HarperCollins, 1998.

Cohen, David. *The Secret Language of the Mind*. San Francisco: Chronicle Books, 1996.

Cryer, Debby. *Active Learning for Infants*. New York: Addison-Wesley Publishing Co., 1987.

Dawson, Geraldine, and Kurt W. Fischer. *Human Behavior and the Developing Brain*. New York: Guilford, 1994.

Diamond, M. *Enriching Heredity: The Impact of the Environment on the Anatomy of the Brain*. New York: Free Press, 1998.

Diamond, Marian, Ph.D., and Janet Hopson. *Magic Trees of the Mind: How to Nurture Your Child's Intelligence, Creativity, and Healthy Emotions from Birth Through Adolescence*. New York: Dutton, 1998.

Doman, Glenn, and Janet Doman. *How to Multiply Your Baby's Intelligence*. Garden City Park, N.Y.: Avery Publishing Group, 1994.

Gardner, Howard. *Frames of Mind*. New York: Basic Books, 1985.

Gibson, Kathleen, and Anne Peterson, eds. *Brain Maturation and Cognitive Development: Comparative and Cross-Cultural Perspectives*. New York: Aldine de Gruyter, 1991.

Goleman, Daniel, Ph.D. *Emotional Intelligence*. New York: Bantam Books, 1995.

Grasselli, Rose N., and Priscilla A. Hegner. *Playful Parenting: Games to Help Your Infants and Toddlers Grow Physically, Mentally, and Emotionally*. New York: Richard Marek Publishers, 1981.

Greenfield, Patricia Marks. *Mind and Media: The Effects of Television, Video Games, and Computers.* Cambridge, Mass.: Harvard University Press, 1984.

Greenspan, Stanley, I., M. D., and Nancy Thorndike Greenspan. *First Feelings: Milestones in the Emotional Development of Your Baby and Child.* New York: Penguin USA, 1994.

Gregory, R. L., ed. *The Oxford Companion to the Mind.* New York: Oxford University Press, 1987.

Gross, Jacquelyn. *Make Your Child a Lifelong Reader.* Los Angeles: Jeremy P. Tarcher, 1986.

Healy, Jane M., Ph.D. *Your Child's Growing Mind: A Practical Guide to Brain Development and Learning from Birth to Adolescence.* New York: Doubleday, 1994.

Holt, John. *How Children Learn.* Reading, Mass.: Addison-Wesley, 1995.

Hooper, J., and D. Teresi. *The Three-Pound Universe.* New York: Macmillan, 1986.

Howard, Pierce J., Ph.D. *The Owner's Manual for the Brain: Everyday Applications from Mind-Brain Research.* Austin, Tex.: Leornian Press, 1994.

Hunt, M. *The Universe Within.* New York: Simon & Schuster, 1982.

Jacob, S. H. *Your Baby's Mind.* Holbrook, Mass.: Adams Media Corp., 1992.

Johnson, Mia. *Teach Your Child to Draw: Bringing Out Your Child's Talents and Appreciation for Art.* Los Angeles: Lowell House, 1990.

Kaplan, Louise. *Oneness and Separateness: From Infant to Individual.* New York: Simon & Schuster, 1998.

Khalsa, Dharma Singh, M. D. *Brain Longevity: Regenerate Your Concentration, Energy, and Learning Ability for a Lifetime of Peak Mental Performance.* New York: Warner Books, 1997.

Kopp, Claire B. *Baby Steps: The "Whys" of Your Child's Behavior in the First Two Years.* New York: W. H. Freeman & Co., 1993.

Lappe, Frances Moore. *What to Do After You Turn Off the TV.* New York: Ballantine, 1985.

Leach, Penelope. *Your Baby and Child: From Birth to Age Five.* New York: Knopf, 1997.

Ludington-Hoe, Susan, and Susan Golant. *How to Have a Smarter Baby*. New York: Bantam Books, 1985.

Mark, Vernon H., M. D., and Jeffrey P. Mark. *Brain Power: A Neurosurgeon's Complete Program to Maintain and Enhance Brain Fitness Throughout Your Life*. Boston: Houghton Mifflin, 1989.

Mehler, Jacques, and Emmanuel Depoux. *What Infants Know: The New Cognitive Science of Early Development*. Cambridge, Mass.: Blackwell Publishers, 1994.

Mike, John, M. D. *Brilliant Babies, Powerful Adults: Awaken the Genius Within*. Clearwater, Fla.: Satori Press International, 1997.

Montessori, Maria, and John Chattin-McNichols. *The Absorbent Mind*. New York: Henry Holt & Co., 1995.

Oberlander, June R. *Slow and Steady Get Me Ready: 260 Weekly Developmental Activities from Birth to Age 5*. Fairfax Station, Va.: Bio-Alpha, Inc., 1992.

Philadelphia Child Guidance Center. *Your Child's Emotional Health: The Early Years*. New York: Macmillan, 1994.

Pinker, Steven. *The Language Instinct*. New York: Morrow, 1994.

Polonsky, Lydia, et al. *Math for the Very Young*. New York: Wiley, 1995.

Restak, Richard M. *The Infant Mind*. Garden City, N.Y.: Doubleday, 1986.

Shelov, Steven P., M. D., ed. *The American Academy of Pediatrics: The Complete and Authoritative Guide to Caring for Your Baby and Young Child: Birth to Age 5*. New York: Bantam, 1998.

Singer, Dorothy G., Jerome L. Singer, and Daina M. Zuckerman. *Use TV to Your Child's Advantage: The Parent's Guide*. Washington, D.C.: Acropolis, 1990.

Suzuki, Shinichi. *Nurtured by Love: A New Approach to Education*. Pompano Beach, Fla.: Exposition Press of Florida, 1982.

Thompson, Richard F. *The Brain: A Neuroscience Primer*. New York: Freeman, 1993.

Trelease, Jim. *The New Read-Aloud Handbook*. New York: Penguin, 1989.

Van de Carr, Rene, and Marc Lehrer. *Prenatal Classroom: A Parent's Guide for Teaching Your Baby in the Womb*. Atlanta: Humanics Learning, 1992.

Warner, Sally. *Encouraging the Artist in Your Child*. New York: St. Martin's Press, 1989.

Weiner, Harvey S. *Talk with Your Child: How to Develop Reading and Language Skills Through Conversation at Home*. New York: Viking, 1988.

White, Burton. *Educating the Infant and Toddler*. New York: Lexington, 1998.

Wilson, Frank R. *Tone Deaf and All Thumbs? An Invitation to Musical-Making for Late Bloomers and Non-Prodigies*. New York: Viking, 1986.

Winter, A., and R. Winter. *Eat Right, Be Bright*. New York: St. Martin's Press, 1988.

Yepsen, R. B., Jr. *How to Boost Your Brain Power: Achieving Peak Intelligence, Memory and Creativity*. Emmaus, Pa.: Rodale, 1987.

ARTICLES

Adamson-Macedo, Elvidina N., et. al. "A Small Sample Follow-up Study of Children Who Received Tactile Stimulation After Preterm Birth: Intelligence and Achievements." *Journal of Reproductive and Infant Psychology* 11, no. 3 (1993): 165–68.

Bell, S. M., and M. D. S. Ainsworth. "Infant Crying and Maternal Responsiveness." *Child Development* 43 (1972): 1171–90.

Benbow, Camilla P., and Julian C. Stanley. "Intellectually Talented Students: Family Profiles." *Gifted Child Quarterly* 24 (Summer 1980): 119–22.

Blann, Randy. "Brain Food: How to Eat Smart." *Psychology Today*, May/June 1996, 35–37.

Bradley, R., and B. Caldwell. "The Relation of Infants' Home Environments to Achievement Test Performance in First Grade: A follow-up Study." *Child Development* 55 (1984): 803–9.

Brown, J. Larry, and Laura Sherman. "The Relationship Between Undernutrition and Behavioral Development in Children." *Journal of Nutrition* 125 (1995): 2281S–84S.

Cohen, Sarale E., and Leila Beckwith. "Preterm Infant Interaction with the Caregiver in the First Year of Life and Competence at Age Two." *Child Development* 50 (1979): 767–76.

Crinic, L. S. "Effects of Nutrition and Environment on Brain Biochemistry and Behavior." *Developmental Psychology* 16, no. 2 (March 1983): 129–45.

DeCasper, A. J., and W. P. Fifer. "Of Human Bonding: Newborns Prefer Their Mothers' Voices." *Science,* 6 June 1980, 1174–76.

DeCasper, A. J., and A. D. Sigafoos. "The Intrauterine Heartbeat: A Potent Reinforcer for Newborns." *Infant Behavior and Development* 6 (1983): 19–25.

Denham, S., and S. Renwick. "Working and Playing Together: Prediction of Preschool Social-Emotional Competence from Mother-Child Interaction." *Child Development* 62 (1991): 242–49.

Detterman, D. K. "The Effect of Heartbeat Sound on Neonatal Crying." *Infant Behavior and Development* 1 (1978): 36–48.

Dwyer, J. "Impact of Maternal Nutrition on Infant Health." *Medical Times* 3, no. 7 (July 1983): 30–38.

Kolata, G. "Studying Learning in the Womb." *Science,* 20 July 1984: 302–3.

Ling, D., and A. Ling. "Communication Development in the First Three Years of Life." *Journal of Speech and Hearing Research* 17 (1974): 146–59.

Pollitt, E., R. L. Leibel, and D. Greenfield. "Brief Fasting, Stress, and Cognition in Children." *American Journal of Clinical Nutrition* 34 (1981): 1526–33.

Ratner, H. "Memory Demands and the Development of Young Children's Memory." *Child Development* 55 (1984): 2173–91.

Rausch, C. B. "Effects of Tactile Kinesthetic Stimulation on Premature Infants." *Journal of Gynecological Nursing* 10, no. 10 (1981): 34–40.

Rausher, Frances H., Gordon L. Shaw, and Katherine N. Ky. "Music and Spatial Task Performance." *Nature* 365 (1993): 611.

Rosenthal, M. K. "Vocal Dialogues in Neonatal Period." *Developmental Psychology* 18 no. 1 (1982): 17–21.

Salk, L. "The Role of the Heartbeat in the Relations Between Mother and Infant." *Scientific American* 220 (1973): 24–29.

Scibetta, J. J., et. al. "Human Fetal Brain Response to Sound During Labor." *American Journal of Obstetrics and Gynecology* 109, no. 1 (1971): 82–85.

Siegel, L. "Reproductive, Perinatal and Environmental Factors as Predictors of the Cognitive and Language Development of Preterm and Full-term Infants." *Child Development* 53 (1982): 963–73.

Swift, E. W., et. al. "Predictive Value of Early Testing of Auditory Localization for Language Development." *Developmental Medicine and Child Neurology* 23, no. 3 (July 1981): 306–16.

Tulkin, Steven R., and Jerome Kagan. "Mother-Child Interaction in the First Year of Life." *Child Development* 53 (1972): 677–86.

Van de Carr, Rene, and Marc Lehrer. "Enhancing Early Speech, Parental Bonding, and Infant Physical Development Using Prenatal Intervention in Standard Obstetric Practices." *Pre- and Peri-Natal Psychology* 1 (Spring 1986): 22–30.

Wynn, M., and A. Wynn. "The Importance of Maternal Nutrition in the Weeks Before and After Conception." *Birth* 9, no. 1 (Spring 1982): 39–43.